DATING
Is Not for Marriage

*Revolutionize How You Date
With Three Simple Questions*

JASON FANNING

Copyright © 2016 by Jason Fanning

Dating Is Not for Marriage
Revolutionize How You Date With Three Simple Questions
by Jason Fanning

Printed in the United States of America.

ISBN 9781498472296

All rights reserved solely by the author. The author guarantees all contents are original and do not infringe upon the legal rights of any other person or work. No part of this book may be reproduced in any form without the permission of the author. The views expressed in this book are not necessarily those of the publisher.

Unless otherwise indicated, Scripture quotations taken from the English Standard Version (ESV). Copyright © 2001 by Crossway, a publishing ministry of Good News Publishers. Used by permission. All rights reserved.

www.xulonpress.com

"We all agree that marriages are in trouble. We all admit that marriages are begun in dating, that dating is primitive, and that Christian singles have emulated the world. So how should dating be perceived? Jason Fanning doesn't give rules as much as the underlying perception one should have of one of our society's most dangerous of territories. I heartily recommend."

—Tom Nelson, senior pastor at Denton Bible Church in Denton, Texas. He is the author of *The Book of Romance*

"In his book, *Dating's Not for Marriage,* Jason Fanning takes us on a provocatively candid journey of his own life story while forcing the reader to take his or her own journey through Scripture and self-discovery. Prepare to have all of your motivations for and assumptions about dating challenged and sharpened. Fanning shares intensely practical insights—from his wealth of pastoral and counseling experience with youth and young adults—in a refreshingly honest and relatable style. The interactive portions of the book will allow you to revisit and share with others all that you discovered about God's Word, your heart, and His will for you and relationships in the days and years to come. The three self-diagnostic questions posed in *Dating's Not for Marriage* are revealing, revolutionary, and indispensable. It's an easy yet essential read for any person who desires to be well informed and equipped to wisely navigate the treacherous world of dating."

>—Andy Vanderveer, student ministry director at Faith Bible Church in Bryan, Texas

"In a world where relationships and marriage are definitely a challenge, Jason offers a fresh perspective of interacting with the scripture, God's love letter. He helps prepare you to no longer live in fear of the wrong relationship, but to be ready for the right one. This book will be a great encouragement for your future mate."

>—Keith Chancey, president of the Kanakuk Institute and director of Kanakuk K-Seven

TABLE OF CONTENTS

FOREWORD xiii
By Tedashii

SECTION 1 16
Setting The Stage

SECTION 2 48
The Three Question Gauntlet

SECTION 3 132
A New Perspective

To Brittany...
You are the woman of my dreams, my best friend, and my greatest encouragement. Thank you for displaying daily God's grace to me.

To Brandon...
A friend as you, I don't deserve.
Thank you for always being in my corner.

To Joe...
My mentor and my friend, thank you for personifying 1 Thess 2 for me.
I'll always be grateful.

ACKNOWLEDGMENTS

Where do I even begin to list the names of the people who formulated this book with me? Those of you who sat with me weekly in your high school days, thank you for letting me into your life. To the leaders I serve and have served alongside, the mentors who spoke truth to me, and many others, I thank you. Because of you this book took shape, and because of you I am encouraged to write.

To the incredible staff I serve and have served alongside, you challenge me daily in ministry. I am surrounded by some of the best people in the world and all have become dear friends. I am honored to be in the trenches with you.

For those who spent countless hours helping me along the way, I thank you. Sarah Atwater, Alexis Airington, Robin Koehn, Resa Curbo, Eddie Renz, Samantha Pfaffly, Parker Metcalf, Erin Newton, Andy Vanderveer, Charles Stolfus, Tom Nelson, John Brown, Danny Falcone, and many others, thank you for your time and for helping me to clearly articulate the thoughts in my brain.

Tedashii, thanks for taking the time to be a part of this book. Your friendship is so valuable to me.

Brandon, you are the best friend all best friends long to have. Thank you for being that to me.

Joe, you have contributed to my life in ways no one else has. Thank you for always being my number-one fan.

Brittany, I have no greater love than you on this earth. You are my dream come true. Thank you for reading and rereading this book more than I did. Thank you.

FOREWORD
By Tedashii

To most this is a book about dating-- you can almost feel the romance in the air as you read through the grand articulation of certain illustrations, the tone, the language, the imagery, the mood, (all things to pay close attention to), even the heart behind every word. But it's not a book about dating. It's about so much more. It's about misconceptions more than misconduct. It's about misunderstandings more than misbehavior. It's a book about awareness more than activity. It's about your affections much more than being affectionate. In a nutshell, it's a book about the heart: the posture and propensity of the heart. And yet, it's about how you engage the heart, your own or someone else's. And I say engage because it relates to the idea of getting someone's attention and occupying their time, in the hopes that it would lead to something more. It's about venturing into the unknown and removing the guesswork we often use to make decisions in dating. You know, guesswork.

My guesswork was always based on what I felt. Sure, I factored in other things to reassure my guesstimates-- attraction, personality, compatibility, and other surface level characteristics—however, I knew "If I wasn't feeling it, then I wasn't feeling it". Which loosely translated into,

"If the feeling isn't strong enough to keep me, then they weren't worth being kept". That sounds harsh, but don't be so quick to judge because I was only doing what we all do when it comes to dating. We base everything on emotion and then wait for the other to affirm or nullify what we feel. That's what I call guesswork. It's not knowing an answer and following a hunch on what you should do. And for most, we affirm the notion of dating someone based on how we feel or are made to feel. Sound familiar? Well it definitely was my story.

So, I did what most do. I implemented rules or a set of guidelines into the equation. Safeguards to keep me from wandering too far from my desires. With boldness, I ventured more into dating only to see not even my rules could get me the answers I was seeking. The more I dated the more I realized how far I was from the path I set out on. This is where most, like I did, get caught up in serial dating. Dating over and over, going from one relationship to the next, with no direction or purpose. It is solely and selfishly based on how the other makes you feel. And in the end it usually leads to more heartache than happiness. This was me, and it was in no way a means to what I truly desired. I began to wonder, "What's the point of this whole thing?" I questioned if what I was doing was actually working. And in this a wonderful reality came to be-- I let go of my truth and began to trust in the Truth. The truth was God had me right where he wanted me. In a place of humility and trust. In a place where I had no clue what to do. It was there I had to admit, "I don't know." I didn't have the answer and I needed Him to show me what I should do, in every area of life, even in dating.

We all need to have that moment. The moment where a light goes off in our heads and we can see clearly that we don't have all the answers and we need someone that does. Where we can finally say, "I don't know how this all works," and bravely admit we're just guessing trying to figure this thing out. What Freedom! And to me this book is a fantastic tool in helping us find that freedom. It helps you begin to remove the guesswork and not let your obscure emotions be the litmus test in dating. So many date like flipping channels on the tv; we look till we like, stay till it's over, and then move on. But people, made in God's image, deserve so much more. I believe God has not left us alone when it comes to this issue, and I'm confident that this book will help anyone that is habitually going from one channel to the next.

So I encourage you to dive in, take your time, remove any distractions, sit with each question intently, and read the burden of a man who desperately desires to see people pursue dating with the heart we were intended to. As I told you, this is a book about the heart so I pray your heart is radically changed as you take on the challenge of learning why dating is not for marriage.

– Tedashii, Hip-Hop artist, radio personality, public speaker {www.tedashii.com}

SECTION 1

SETTING THE STAGE

UNDERSTANDING THIS BOOK

About the Author

As I looked out into the crowd, I realized I was living a dream. It was a surreal feeling to have my older brother at my side and some of my closest friends standing behind him. My mentor, Joe, stood in front of me and peered down the same aisle as I did. This is the day of which every person hopes to be a part. This is a day when emotions run high, jitters flow rapidly, and expectations become realities.

Everyone in the room stood. My brother glanced at me and then fixed his eyes down the vacant aisle, which was filled with red rose petals. As that familiar music began everyone looked to the doors as they flew open. Her beautiful white dress filled the entryway. Our guests were on their feet before Joe could even call their attention to her entrance.

I still can't remember when I knew it was real. I can't even remember much of that day at all, other than a feeling of grace perfectly combined with joy. The moment came as her father placed her hand in mine. I felt a type of excitement I rarely feel. From then on it was a whirlwind. Before I knew it, I was reading the vows we had written. Maybe that is the part I remember most.

The gravity of wedding vows sometimes slips our minds when we hear them spoken, but when face to face with a future spouse, they are powerful coming from one's own mouth. Brittany and I spent a lot of time writing those vows. When I say we spent *a lot* of time, I am not referring to one sitting. We spent most of our dating time writing those vows—we just didn't know it.

We wrote those lines through decisions we faced, temptations we felt, and experiences we shared. Our vows were a result of who we were as a couple and how God molded us together. Our vows came from the sanctifying experiences of dating and engagement. They came from the joy, laughter, and excitement we shared getting to know each other.

As I read those lines, I realized what it meant to be married. I realized my successes and failures in dating. As I read those lines, I realized my love for my Savior is reflected in my love for my wife. Our vows read as follows:

I, Jason/Brittany, promise to love and respect you, Brittany/Jason, in ways beyond my own ability, through God's grace alone.

I promise to joyfully lead you in every aspect of life as is glorifying to our King, serving you as Jesus served the Church, even unto death.

I will strive to be Christ to you by counting you greater than myself, just as Jesus counted me on the Cross. Forsaking all others, I will pursue you for the rest of our lives, as God in Christ has pursued me.

I promise to love you as my own body, which is no longer my own.

Understanding This Book

I promise to look to your interests as greater than mine, through patience, kindness, forgiveness, sacrifice, protection, and service.

I promise to cherish you and cling to our friendship in times of trial and of peace.

The topic of dating is close to my heart because I believe it exposes nerves in our souls that draw us close to Christ more so than most other things we go through. Ultimately this results in the honoring of our Savior in marriage. My hope and prayer is that by exploring the three major questions I offer in this book, you might see dating in a much different light than you did before. I hope that this Three Question Gauntlet will revolutionize how you date.

I am currently the student ministry director at Denton Bible Church in Texas. I get the privilege of shepherding students in sixth through twelfth grades every year, alongside our incredible staff and volunteer leaders. I am a graduate of the University of North Texas and received my master's degree from Dallas Theological Seminary.

I am the husband of Brittany Fanning, who is far greater than any wife I could have ever imagined. I am the father to two incredible boys. My family is my greatest hobby. Brittany and I enjoy the simple things in life. Our ideal night probably includes some cold Texas weather, sitting next to a warm fire, curling up with our pets and kids, playing a game, or watching some random television show. We love to laugh and share our lives with others.

I never set out to be a student pastor or write a book. God had plans for me I never had the nerve to dream. Both just fell into my lap.

I am one of the lucky ones, growing up with incredible parents who feared the Lord and introduced me to Him at an early age. I would have told you back then that I was a Christian, but I truly believe God called me to Himself when I was seventeen years old. Early in my life, I associated my Christianity with who my parents were, the church I went to, and the amount of good things I did. It was my junior year of high school when the truth of the Gospel was illumined to me, and I placed my faith in Jesus.

The fun part of my story starts right after my freshman year of college when I returned home to Texas after failing as a collegiate golfer. When I returned home at age nineteen, my best friend, Brandon, and I started a golf business making custom golf clubs and repairing golf clubs. If you can't play it, why not make money at it?

During this time the Lord had turned my heart's desire fully to Him. It has been said that Christians experience two different parts to their lives. One is when they view the cross, realize the sacrifice Jesus made, and place their faith in Him. The second is when they visit the tomb, and, like Thomas, see the wound, and then serve the Lord in a way they had never served before.

I was nineteen the year I saw the wounds. For the first time, I sought what God had in store for my life. This led me to entertain an invitation from an old friend to volunteer with the middle school ministry at Denton Bible Church. This was the beginning of a huge life change for me. I heard my calling.

After a few successful years in our golf business, an investor approached Brandon and me with an idea that required us to sell our current business and go into partnership with him. When it came time to sell the business, I told Brandon I wanted to work part time in the student ministry at our church to see what it was like. I wanted to see the inside, the dirt, the politics, or whatever it was those church people dealt with. I was hired as the part-time trips and events coordinator for Denton Bible

Student Ministries. And as I saw all of the difficult and shocking parts of ministry, I only fell in love with it more.

Before we continue let me warn you, I am a *The Lord of the Rings* geek. Bear with me. If you are not familiar with the movie or books, shame on you. Just kidding. Let me introduce two characters to you: 1) Arwen is an elf woman, who is able to have eternal life by sailing away on a magical ship. 2) Aragorn is a mortal man she falls in love with, but in order to stay and marry him, Arwen has to give up her immortal life.

As Arwen heads off to the ship, she realizes her love for Aragorn and sees their future together. Their future involves death. It involves her being mortal. If she chooses to stay and marry him, she forfeits the comfort of knowing her destiny. She utters a life-altering line shortly after: "I choose a mortal life." To those around her, this decision is absurd. But to her it is the best decision she could make, her *only* choice.

As dorky as this is, I remember pacing around my backyard in Denton. I was fidgeting with a knot that had fallen out of our raggedy, wooden fence. I prayed about what to do. *Should I stay in the business world, or give it all up and go into ministry?* After praying for some time, I took the piece of wood I was fidgeting with and wrote in black Sharpie, "I choose a mortal life."

To me, this was a way of saying that I would not take the safe way, that my destiny was now more unknown. I was willing to jump into the unknown and do what I love. My father always told me, "Son, do what you love. Money will come." I took his advice that day.

I remember wondering what my family would think or if Brandon would be upset with me. Thankfully all were supportive when I broke the news. I told Brandon I would not be a part of the new business because God was clearly and relentlessly calling me into student ministry. I called our investor and told him the same. From that day forward, my life in the business world was over.

I started as a volunteer small-group leader and then was hired on a part-time basis to handle events and administration. That was followed by a full-time position as the associate ministry director, and later I was offered the directorial position for the 2013–2014 school year. That was my twelfth school year serving at Denton Bible Student Ministries in various capacities.

The Intention of this Book

It was a warm summer day in Denton, Texas, as I tried to outsmart the nasty traffic by the local mall. I thought I would take a back road past the new hospital and cheat that awful mall traffic. I guess I was not the only one who had this brilliant idea. I sat through at least three or four lights, just trying to make it near the hospital. I still had not made it through the stoplight.

About that time I looked in my rearview mirror and saw some "jerk" driving on the shoulder to pass all the other cars. Anger built in me as I watched this man fly past all of us good citizens who waited our turn at the light. I was briefly distracted by the sound of an oncoming CareFlight helicopter that flew directly over my truck on its way to the hospital. I watched it for a few seconds and then caught another glimpse of this maniac going around all the traffic.

Cars honked, and angry fists flew out windows toward this man. I am usually a pretty calm driver, but this day I decided to take matters into my own hands. I decided I would be a bigger jerk. I inched up as far as I could into the shoulder, leaving my lane to cut off this man so he could not pass my truck in his attempt to cheat the traffic situation. I had sat in the thick of the tangle for what seemed

Understanding This Book

like forever, and no way was I going to let this man get away with this.

I remember feeling the awkwardness of the man pulling up right beside me. I embraced that awkwardness and had my stare ready for him when he pulled up. I was shocked by the look on his face. It was not anger. It was terror. He motioned for me to roll down my passenger side window, and I was ready for a fight! I rolled it down and got the first words out by exclaiming, "Can I help you with something?"

"I just need to get by," he replied.

"We all need to get by," I answered.

His final reply left me speechless.

"Yes, I know you do sir, but I need to get by because that's my son in there." He pointed toward the CareFlight helicopter that had just flown past as it was landing on the pad next to the emergency room. Humiliated I pulled my truck into the ditch. Silence.

In an instant my perspective changed. The way I viewed this man as I saw him approaching changed by the time I watched him leave. It just took a little information about his motivation for passing me to change my view of him. It took a moment of seeing his heart to change the way I viewed his actions. I hope this book does the same for you when it comes to your view of dating relationships. I hope this book forces you to look into your motivation and your heart.

Over and over I hear students, volunteer leaders, and anyone who is not married asking about dating relationships. I love this subject because I have found nothing that gets us to the reality of our hearts quicker than the subject of dating. It exposes us emotionally, physically, spiritually, and socially. It exposes our hearts like few things can. This is why I wanted to write this book—to help us search our hearts.

This book is not intended to fix your relationships. Nor is this book intended to help you get a date. This book really is not even intended to make your relationship better. This book is intended to force you to search your own heart and consider why. This is the question no one is asking. The question of why we are making the decisions we are making, or why we are doing the things we are doing. This book is meant to inspire you to question if you are in a position to be dating in the first place.

My motivation for this book can be compared to the legalization of pot. Yes, I mean the drug. Let me explain. I was sitting in a classroom with a pastor on staff named Charles. Charles is the intellectual type, with an uncanny ability to engage you in a debate without your even knowing it.

In this particular class, the topic of legalizing marijuana came up, and his response floored me. Charles explained that as Christians we hold to the belief that drugs such as these are something we should not partake in. He mentioned that the easy answer given for not smoking pot is that it is illegal. While this is a valid reason, this is not the best reason.

If we simply abstain from pot because it is against society's rules, we are not reflecting a regenerated behavior— we are reflecting a legalistic behavior. (Please do not misunderstand me, as I believe obedience to the authorities God has placed in charge is crucial). His point was that if we decide we are not going to smoke pot simply because it is illegal, then we actually are motivated by the external and not the internal.

I think legalization of pot could potentially be a good, convicting challenge for Christians. If pot were legal all over the country, then we as Christians would have to now search our own hearts and make calls based on our individual convictions. No longer are we be able to rely on

Understanding This Book

a rule but rather are forced to search the depths of our beliefs, values, and faith. This is how Christians live!

In the same way, this book encourages the reader to soul-search. I am not here to say you should or should not date. Instead, I hope to inspire you to search your own heart, circumstances, and convictions. I purposely do not give any hard and fast rules for you to follow. I think that is the easy way out. If you are looking for those, there are plenty of great books already out there for you to read.

I have become accustomed to listening to many different single people talk about their love lives and the current romantic drama. They ask these and other questions: "How far is too far?" "How old should I be before I date?" "Do you think I'm ready to date?" "How many dates should we go on in a week?"

Frankly, they are asking the wrong questions. What seems to be missing in our Christian dating culture is not an action issue. We are not missing suggestions, ideas, or strategies. What we are missing is a heart-based issue. We ought to be taking a deep look into our own souls as to why we are doing what we are doing. We should strive for an honest communication with ourselves when it comes to dating. Some overlook major heart issues and go on with dating relationships they now feel ashamed of. This is what drove me to write the book.

Often we search the Internet or bookshelves to help us answer questions about how to act on a date, what time to have her home, how to set boundaries, and so on. The point missing is the "why?" Is it not also important to educate single people on *why* personal boundaries are important? Shouldn't we tell them *why* to give flowers or cards? Couldn't we even ask *why* they like the people they are dating?

This book is intended to deal with the heart of the person. If we build dating relationships on the foundation of rules alone, we conveniently avoid dealing with the *heart* of the issue. Sometimes rules can provide a crutch, which allows us to avoid a deepening in our soul and our dependence on Christ.

This book uses what I call a Three Question Gauntlet as a self-evaluation of your own heart—how to properly view yourself and your dating relationship, and ultimately decide if you should be in one. It also communicates how you can approach dating in a God-glorifying way, starting from the inside. My hope is that this book equips you by walking through three questions to help you self-evaluate if you should be in a dating relationship or how you should approach your current dating relationship. The questions are designed to be a very clear-cut and simple system. If you fail to make it through, you should seriously consider if you should be dating or if you need to make some drastic changes.

This book is an interactive book. There are often places where you need to discover things in Scripture and in your own heart by interacting with questions. Space is provided for you to write in the book as questions and suggestions walk you through the process, step by step. I believe interaction and self-discovery are very important, because when forced to learn something on your own, it tends to stick with you in a more impactful and memorable way.

I have three main hopes for you as you read my book:
1. I hope that by the time you come to the end of this book, you have an understanding of where *you* stand as far as relationships are concerned.
2. I hope you find clarity about whether or not you should be in a relationship, as well as tools to evaluate *your heart* within a relationship.

3. I hope you encounter Jesus in a way you never have before as the Spirit grabs you in such a way that forever changes you.

Getting Personal

I remember sitting under a large tree outside the Denton Courthouse when Brittany and I had just become "Facebook official"—back when all of us were addicted to Facebook. I started where every "good" Christian starts, with the physical boundaries talk. I had my mind made up before we even began that we were not going to kiss until our wedding day. So when we started the conversation, I fired away with this brilliant idea. I was ready for her to shower me with praises of my godliness and wisdom, but she hesitated...and I knew we were not on the same page.

"Really?" she asked. "Not that I'm just dying to kiss you right now, but that just seems a little bit weird to me."

I brilliantly replied, "Uh, I, uh, ya, well, let's just talk about this later then."

I wish you could have seen it—you would still be laughing at me. Let me be clear that if this is your plan, then please stick to it! I have known some very godly couples who have done this, and it worked well for them.

I went home that night and could not stop replaying the short conversation in my head. I sat down with my prayer journal to explore my heart's motivation. *Why* was it I wanted to not kiss until marriage? As I contemplated the "why," I soon realized I was driven by fear. I was afraid we would mess up, and felt it would be easier for me if I just took the option of failing out of play. If failing were not an option, how could I mess up?

At this point, I realized this was about my following a bunch of "rules" so I would never have to deal with my heart. For me, this was the easy way out. By simply not kissing at all, I did not have to deal with my heart or face the possibility of failure. In the end, however, avoiding the heart issue would have made it more difficult for me now.

We had to walk through those things in faith, not fear. When I say "fear," I refer to the absence of faith. There is a very healthy "fear" of sin in regard to susceptibleness to it. And there is a healthy "fear" of who God is. But I am referring to a "fear" of not looking like a "good" Christian on the outside while avoiding the heart behind my decision as seen in Matthew 5:21–24:

You have heard that it was said to those of old, "You shall not murder; and whoever murders will be liable to judgment." But I say to you that everyone who is angry with his brother will be liable to judgment; whoever insults his brother will be liable to the council; and whoever says, "You fool!" will be liable to the hell of fire. So if you are offering your gift at the altar and there remember that your brother has something against you, leave your gift there before the altar and go. First be reconciled to your brother, and then come and offer your gift.

The next day I went to Brittany and talked to her about what I had discovered. I told her I was acting out of fear, not faith, that I was approaching physical boundaries with a legalistic attitude. I told her we needed to set up specific boundaries because I did not trust myself, but that we were going to do this in faith. Now I had a reason to set up boundaries! I realized this was not an effort simply to "not sin," but rather an effort to "be holy." It was not a question of *How can I not mess up?* but a question of *How can I most honor Christ?*

This is the reason for my approach to this book. My prayer is that this book encourages you to act in faith according to the grace of Jesus Christ. If you do not know Him, I pray God might use this book to blow away the fog and illumine Himself to you.

Understanding This Book

Some Ground Rules
1. If you are currently dating someone and you can't see past that person, you might carry a bias that will skew this process.
2. Be honest. We are often the best liars when it comes to lying to ourselves.
3. Take your time. Do not assume you know the answer. Slow down, and search your heart.
4. You are in a relationship that is unique to you. Take this book, and mold it into your own context.

Your Attention, Please

In school, teachers teach that you always need to start your papers with an introduction that is a strong attention-getter. So may I have your attention, please? I mean, come on—if you are a human who breathes oxygen, I probably already got your attention simply by using the word "dating" in my book's title.

Let me paint you a picture. It began in fifth grade. What the heck was I thinking when I asked out that girl in elementary school and almost had a heart attack when the cheek kiss came? Did we really ever go on a date? I don't think it counted as a date when Mommy picked us up and dropped us off at the movie theater—we couldn't see half the movies because we were not even thirteen yet. How embarrassing!

Or how about the sixth-grade girlfriend I wanted to date really badly because my best friend was dating *her* best friend, and man, wouldn't that be fun to hang out together? This was serious—so serious in fact that we even had "our" song. Boy, was that special…or absolutely humiliating?

Then seventh-grade hit. I didn't even know the girl I asked out, but I wanted to go out with her because everybody else thought she was beautiful. Was I serious?

The humiliation continues. The next girl in middle school was interesting. Our relationship consisted of a cycle of breaking up and getting back together. Just before the homecoming dance she dumped me for another guy, and then I won her back right before the homecoming game. Being a clever and thoughtful girlfriend, she took the garter (welcome to Texas) she'd bought for the other guy and rearranged its letters to spell my name! Can you feel my humiliation?

Finally there was the "real" relationship during my latter high school years and into college. I had become a believer during this time, and I thought I had this dating thing down—except for the having-no-idols-before-God thing, the guarding-our-hearts thing, or the leading-of-the-relationship thing. Have I embarrassed myself enough? Maybe you can identify with me just a little bit.

My point is this that I might not know exactly where you are on the dating scene, but I've been there and can relate. I know dating is a difficult road to navigate, so I hope to shine some light on the confusing, exciting, and weird process we all go through.

What if your future dating relationships could *all* be considered successful, even if you were to experience a breakup? What if you could walk down an aisle one day in complete confidence of your decision? If you are honest with yourself, I believe the process outlined in this book will help spare you from a life of misguided relationships.

SETTING A CLEAR GOAL

Brittany and I soon realized we shared a common love. Almost weekly we found our way to sharing in this love by visiting a different California Pizza Kitchen each time we went out on a date. We loved the pizza. I remember dressing in my finest frat-tucked Polo shirt, and my Afro curls had just the right amount of relaxer in them. It was winter, so I was pleased to wear my dad's old, black lizard boots. Needless to say I was ready for our date. I picked up Brittany in my electric-blue 2000 Dodge Sport truck, and off we went to get some pizza. My goal was clear that night—to impress this girl.

When we arrived at the restaurant, we were seated immediately and were brought some of that delicious bread. We knew better than to fill up on the bread while waiting for the pizza, but we indulged anyway. Moments into our pleasant conversation, I anticipated that flavor hitting my tongue as I spread the perfect amount of butter onto a huge piece of the bread. I was starving.

After achieving this buttered perfection, I joyfully brought that bread to my mouth and chomped down as hard as I could. The bread fought back. I was not quite aware that the crust of the bread was as hard as a rock. As I bit down, the bread sliced open the roof of my mouth.

I let out a yelp and instinctively grabbed the napkin, jamming it in my mouth as quickly as possible.

With my tongue holding the napkin to the roof of my mouth, I tried to explain to Brittany what had happened. I failed to make out the proper words, so I resorted to opening and pointing inside my mouth filled with bread, blood, and napkin. I tried to speak the few words needed for her to understand. "I cuwt mwuy mowth," I muttered.

"What?" she replied.

I spoke louder this time, as if volume were the problem. "I cuwt mwuy mowth," I said, opening as wide as I could and pointing to the bloody napkin.

After a few minutes of profuse bleeding and failing to properly explain what had happened, I headed to the bathroom to fix the issue. Ten minutes later I returned to the table, realizing I had not accomplished my goal of impressing this girl. This date was a disaster, or was it?

In daily life you set goals, whether you realize it or not. You might have a goal to pay attention in class, to read a book, to do your homework, or to move up in your current job. You could have a goal to get back in shape and eat more healthy. Whatever your goal, there is an expectation of how that goal will help you in life. Your goals define your success.

It is easy to define success in a business, in a sport, or on a test. But when it comes to dating, what is the goal in a relationship? How do you define success? What about the relationship you are in or want to be in?

Take some time to think about this question: *What is the goal of any dating relationship?* Once you have your answer, formulate that thought into one sentence and write it out in the space below.

_____

_____

My guess is that most people might tend to write down the word "marriage" as the goal of dating—unless you accurately remember the title of this book, of course. If you did write "marriage" or something along the lines of marriage, I challenge you to consider another option. Not that your answer is wrong, but maybe there is another goal to have in mind.

I truly believe "marriage" is not the best answer to the goal of dating. I do not think marriage is the goal of dating; rather, marriage is the *result* of dating. I have no doubt that if you date someone long enough, you will end up married. Marriage is the result, produced over time, of a dating relationship.

The progression of time in a relationship often takes a couple from "dating as friends"—and who can forget the ol' social-media status with the "likes" rolling in?—to eventually ring-shopping because you just have to propose to this girl! This is the typical scenario as to how dating usually plays out in the United States, so to be successful in this process, we must define what the goal of dating is. So what *is* the goal?

What if I were to share that the thought of marriage *not* being the goal was life-changing for me? What if I were to say that if we agree on this goal, it cuts to the very core of our hearts? What if the goal of dating were a *divine* goal? What if the goal of dating were far bigger than you or your romantic partner will ever be? What if the goal of dating were in line with the very purpose for which you were created?

Getting Personal

Before I met my wife, I spent about seven years as a single guy and was proud of it. My roommates and I formed our own childish "no girls allowed" club, which we laughed about on occasion. I enjoyed the single life. I was not looking for someone to date, but of course Brittany changed all of that. After a few months of liking Brittany, I thought more and more about asking her out. She had become much more than just a blip on the radar—she was someone I thought about often. Before I even got serious about asking her out on a date, I had to call for the advice of my mentor, Joe.

My friend Joe was the student ministry director at Denton Bible during this time. Joe was the guy who trained and grounded me in ministry. Each week as I went further and further into uncharted waters, I called Joe for advice. One day as we were talking, he asked me what I had never thought to ask myself: *What's the goal of dating?*

I told him I had no idea what the goal was, and at that point he introduced an analogy that changed my life forever. Joe leveraged my love of relational ministry to help me understand. "Why do you go to all those football games?" he asked.

"I go to hang out with students," I answered.

"That is what you do, but that is not why you go," he replied.

"OK, well, I go so students know I love them," I countered.

"That is a result of going, but that is not why you go," he replied again.

After a few more halfhearted efforts, I gave up. "Then you tell me. *Why* do I go to football games?" I asked, frustration in my voice.

Joe gave me his final answer. "You go to games because, by going to that game, there's a small chance that through it Jesus would be magnified and honored by your presence there. That some student might see you there and, ultimately in his or her heart, know you are there because of your Savior. And that is the exact reason you date."

Joe taught me an invaluable lesson that day. He taught me that we don't date to get married—marriage is a result.

We date to magnify or honor Christ both *in* and *through* our relationships. To magnify, honor or glorify God is the chief end of all people. This is our life's purpose. This brings us ultimate fulfillment, joy and value. A dating relationship is no different.

Paul writes this in Ephesians 5:31–32, concerning marriage:

> *Therefore a man shall leave his father and mother and hold fast to his wife, and the two shall become one flesh. This mystery is profound, and I am saying that it refers to Christ and the church.*

Using the space below, write down what you think Paul is referring to when he says "mystery."

_____

_____

How does marriage represent Christ to the church? Here's a hint in Ephesians 5:25:

Husbands, love your wives, as Christ loved the church and gave himself up for her.

John gives us more insight in Revelation 19:6–8:

Then I heard what seemed to be the voice of a great multitude, like the roar of many waters and like the sound of mighty peals of thunder, crying out, "Hallelujah! For the Lord our God the Almighty reigns. Let us rejoice and exult and give him the glory, for the marriage of the Lamb has come, and his Bride has made herself ready; it was granted her to clothe herself with fine linen, bright and pure."

Considering that Revelation deals with end times, who is the "Lamb" in this text?

___

Who is the "Bride"?

___

So what union does this portray?

___

    The driving force behind what I'm saying is found in the "mystery"—the mystery that God's intent in marriage is to display the relationship between Christ and the church. Marriage is, therefore, an earthly shadow of a divine reality. This is why the Bible speaks of marriage not being needed in heaven, because the thing marriage was meant to be a shadow of will be right in front of us. We will be united with Jesus—the bride (the church) to the bridegroom (Jesus).
    Remember back to the last wedding you attended. You watched the groom stand at the end of the aisle, ready to receive his bride. The groom is the knight in shining armor, waiting to be united with the one he loves. All of a sudden the pastor has you turn to face the bride. She is beautiful, without blemish. She walks down the aisle in her white dress, on the arm of her father. She smiles ear to ear, waiting to be united with her soon-to-be husband. She knows he would lay down his life for her, that he loves her in a way no one has ever loved her before. The groom awaits the same, but in a different way. He joyously awaits the relationship he always dreamed of, the relationship he lived for.

Jesus is this to us. We watch the bridegroom, Jesus, stand in the gap of sin and death. He stands and calls us to Him, to forever be united with Him. He is our knight in shining armor, the one who slays sin and death on a cross, forever conquering what we could not. His love for us is unwavering and unstoppable, so much so that to unite us in relationship with Him, he slays the one thing that separated us—sin.

He slays it by becoming sin on our behalf and absorbing the wrath of God meant for us. He takes our hit, the wrath meant for us. Then he grants us His own righteousness, if we just believe. Upon this confession of faith, He grants us a white garment that symbolizes our righteousness provided through the Son's death on a cross.

His life was lived for this relationship, and his life was laid down so it could be complete. This marriage, this good news, is that we have relationship with the Father, through the Son, who has clothed us in righteousness through His resurrection and ascension.

Going Deeper

When you think of the goal in any dating relationship, imagine it through a lens of honoring Christ both *in* and *through* the relationship. Honoring Christ *in* the relationship happens when no one is watching, and honoring Christ *through* the relationship happens when everyone is watching. Our lives are formed around this idea of honoring or bringing glory to God. But don't take my word for it—take these guys'...

Paul says it in 1 Corinthians 6:20 and 10:31:

> *For you were bought with a price. So glorify God in your body.*

> So, whether you eat or drink, or whatever you do, do all to the glory of God.

Isaiah says it in Isaiah 43:7:

> Everyone who is called by my name,
> whom I created for my glory,
> whom I formed and made.

Paul says it again in Ephesians 1:3–6:

> Blessed be the God and Father of our Lord Jesus Christ, who has blessed us in Christ with every spiritual blessing in the heavenly places, even as he chose us in him before the foundation of the world, that we should be holy and blameless before him. In love he predestined us for adoption as sons through Jesus Christ, according to the purpose of his will, to the praise of his glorious grace, with which he has blessed us in the Beloved.

Peter says it in 1 Peter 3:15:

> But in your hearts honor Christ the Lord as holy, always being prepared to make a defense to anyone who asks you for a reason for the hope that is in you; yet do it with gentleness and respect.

Matthew quotes Jesus, saying it in Matthew 5:16:

> In the same way, let your light shine before others, so that they may see your good

Setting A Clear Goal

works and give glory to your Father who is in heaven.

These are just a few obvious Bible verses in which we can see that bringing honor and glory to God is what life is all about.

I was meeting with a student, a great kid who loved the Lord, and he recently had started dating a girl. I was talking to him about this, and we discussed what it means to honor Christ *in* a relationship. I asked him what his physical boundaries were and why he had them. He told me the details, saying that making out was as far as they would go. I tried not to show my surprise, continuing the conversation.

"Cool, man," I said. "So how did you guys come to perceive that as something that honors Christ?"

"Well," he responded, "whenever we make out, it just brings us closer together. We just feel like we have a stronger bond, and are a closer brother and sister in Christ."

Although a little surprised, I calmly replied, "Hey, pray about those boundaries specifically, and when we meet again next week, I would love to chat more about it."

When I left Chick-fil-A that day, I wanted to kick myself. Why didn't I push back more on this issue? He clearly was in the wrong, and I did not take a stand. I was ready to confront him the next week, when we met for breakfast at that same Chick-fil-A.

Before I could say anything, he began, "Hey, before we do anything, I've got to talk to you straight-up. Making out with my girlfriend is not honoring to Christ at all. As a matter of fact, it is not honoring to her either. The only person it is honoring to is me. We do not make out anymore."

I was all smiles. That was the Spirit at work in his life. The Spirit created a "game plan" of how best to honor Christ *in* their relationship when no one else was watching. This student was beginning to understand that the goal of his relationship was to honor Christ and not himself. Like this student, your goal is to honor Christ *in* your relationship. This gives reason to put things like boundaries into relationships, and gives purpose to things always assumed to be the right thing to do.

While your goal is to honor Christ *in* your relationship, it must also be to honor Christ *through* your relationship. Here is what I mean: Do you have that friend who, every time he or she gets into a relationship, falls off the face of the earth? He or she ditches you every time you want to hang out, and then calls you after a fight with him or her and expects you to console? This is the guy or girl who only hangs out with you when he or she cannot hang out with the boy or girl. Have you ever met that couple before? Situations like these are not honoring to Christ *through* the relationship. To honor Christ *through* the relationship means you both put on Christ and display Him to others.

Here is an example of a great way to honor Christ through a relationship: A friend was dating a girl whose roommate was single. Many of their friends were getting married, and these were two of the last among their social group who was not yet engaged. One night my friend talked to his girlfriend about their Valentine's Day plans, and he threw out an idea that had the potential to blow up in his face.

He asked what she thought about inviting her roommate on their Valentine's date with them. He was fearful this might offend her or feel as if he did not really care for her, but her reaction was the opposite. She was thrilled with the gesture, that they could honor Christ by bringing her friend along with them. When Valentine's Day rolled around, he walked up to the door with two cards and two bouquets of roses. After he handed the first set of gifts to his girlfriend, he walked past her and handed her roommate the second set. As the roommate read the card, she realized she was also being taken out on a Valentine's date that happened to be at her favorite restaurant. She was ecstatic.

This story is a great example of one couple who, by God's grace, saw an opportunity to use their relationship in honoring their Savior. Jesus was honored *through* their relationship that night.

In and *Through*

Think of some ways you can honor Christ both *in* and *through* your relationship. If you are not currently in a relationship, look back to one in the past or to the one you dream of in the future. Let's start with *in*, which pertains to when no one is looking. Take a few minutes to write down seven of your own ideas on how you can bring glory and honor to Jesus *in* your dating relationship:

1. _____

2. _____

3. _____

4. _____

5. _____

6. _____

7. _____

I could list off ideas of my own here, but for your sake, I won't. I would rather you wrestle with your own heart and feel the Spirit's conviction in you. Sometimes we think that if we can just follow a formulaic list of rules, then God will be pleased with us and "bless" our relationship so we never break up. But that is not necessarily the case.

Now think about honoring Christ *through* the relationship. How can you reflect Him to others? How can you display a relationship full of love, selflessness, God-centeredness, and honesty for others to see? List out, here, five ways you can do that:

1. _____

2. _____

3. _____

4. _____

5. _____

Now just for fun, do the opposite. Take a few minutes to write down a list of seven things you might do that are *not* honoring to Christ *in* or *through* your relationship: (HINT: to honor Christ means we are trusting Him, delighting in Him, following Him, obeying His Word, submitting to His will, etc.)

1. _____

2. _____

3. _____

Setting A Clear Goal

4. _____

5. _____

6. _____

7. _____

Are there things in your current relationship you need to immediately change? If so, first hold on and finish this book. If you simply change because you feel guilty right now, then you are again missing the point. I am not just talking about a change in your actions—I am talking about a change in your heart.

Imagine if we were to change the goal of our dating relationships from marriage to honoring Christ. This small shift in our minds frees us from the pressures of being the "perfect couple" and making sure we always look good on the outside. This shift trades an inward focus on self to that of a loving Savior. It moves past our own abilities, and all the focus turns to our reliance on Christ.

When honoring Christ is the goal, a breakup is not considered failure if the best decision is to honor our Savior. You no longer feel like your life is over if you "lose" someone, because you simply know you are acting in faith in honoring our King. When honoring Christ is the goal, a relationship has few regrets. When honoring Christ is the goal, you do not have to worry about avoiding sin but rather pursuing righteousness as given by Christ. You no longer wait up at night for that last text, so you can sleep easy at night. You no longer worry about how much someone likes you that day.

The freedom Christ offers is absolutely amazing. We gain this freedom in Christ by trusting Him. My point is simple. The goal of dating is to honor Christ both *in* and *through* the relationship.

Getting Personal

It was Valentine's Day 2009, and I fell into the trap of doing what the holiday demanded I do. I dreaded the amount of money I would have to spend to buy roses for Brittany. I had so many doubts bouncing around in my head. *Does she even like roses? Are roses too common? Should I get some other type of flower? Didn't someone tell me red communicates I'm in love already?* I debated for weeks, feeling like I would fail no matter what. I actually put off buying anything until the day before Valentine's Day and finally randomly drove by a tent outside of Kroger with roses for sale. I swung by and bought whatever I could and then went inside to buy a card.

I had to pick the perfect card, as well—nothing too "lovey" but also not too vague. After I found the perfect card, I did not know what to write in the card. *Should I tell her all my feelings or leave some in suspense?* I spent hours putting together twelve flowers and a piece of paper with colorful ink on it, half with excitement and half with worry. My actions that day were motivated by obligation and panic.

The next day as I drove to her house to pick her up, I felt an overwhelming sense of guilt as I looked at those roses. I really didn't buy those roses with her in mind but with *me* in mind. My heart's intent had nothing to do with the implications of the gospel in my life but everything to do with impressing my girlfriend. I wanted her to think I was romantic, thoughtful, and selfless. I wanted her to be impressed with me.

When I pulled into her driveway, I hesitated before going to the door. You would have thought I was about

Setting A Clear Goal

to ask her out for the first time. I took a few minutes to search my heart, praying God would remove my selfish motivation and replace it with selfless, God-centered motivation. I sat, reflecting on my sin and insecurities. I had lost the goal I once had. Days before, my goal was to simply honor Christ, but in this moment I was honoring me. I sought the Lord and begged Him to change my heart, and He did. I walked to the door and handed her the roses, with a heart of serving and not of impressing others. She never knew the difference, but I did.

This perspective changes everything! Think about it. If my goal is to honor Christ *in* my relationship, this gives me reason to place the infamous "physical boundaries." These boundaries are not about how far is too far or how close can I get without sinning. These boundaries are set because of my love for my Savior, because I know I want to honor him when no one else is watching.

Think about your own Valentine's Day experience. Some people fear Valentine's Day. Immediately one thinks of flowers, chocolates, cards, cologne, a big date, money, expectations, and, of course, Hallmark, but I'll bet you have never thought about the "why?" *Why* do you spend hours at that creepy cologne place in the mall looking for the perfect gift for him? *Why* do you buy her the perfect bouquet of red roses? If you were honest, you would say you do this out of obligation or as a means of preventive maintenance so it does not result in disappointment or anger. Is this honoring to Jesus, to the one Paul speaks of in Philippians 2 who has a mind of considering others more significant than Himself?

What if you were to go to the mall or florist next Valentine's Day with your new goal in mind? Then you would think of Christ. You would think of His love for us, His perfect obedience to the Father, and His ability to consider others more significant than Himself. He did all of this by placing Himself on a cross, absorbing the wrath of God on our behalf.

What if you could take this heart-based approach of considering others more significant than yourself? That way, when you buy that cologne or those roses, it is not to make him or her like you more, not to manipulate the person into thinking you are sweet, and not out of obligation. Buying a gift is motivated by the heart and simply says, "I want to sacrificially give to my brother or sister in Christ in an effort to display a heart that has been changed by Christ." He or she will never know the difference. But you will.

Reflection Questions

What is the end result of dating?

_____

_____

_____

What is the goal of dating?

_____

_____

_____

Give an example of honoring Christ *in* the relationship:

_____

_____

Setting A Clear Goal

Give an example of honoring Christ *through* the relationship:

_____

_____

_____

What is a step you can take this week to better line up with a God-centered goal of dating?

_____

_____

_____

SECTION 2

THE THREE QUESTION GAUNTLET

THE FIRST QUESTION: THE ONE YOU'VE NEVER ASKED

Throughout my own experience while dating Brittany, I accidentally stumbled across three questions I found extremely helpful. These questions took about a year for me to fully formulate, and they are the basis of this book. I call them the Three Question Gauntlet. It can be difficult to make it through this Gauntlet. Remember, if you cannot make it through after honestly answering the questions, you must ask yourself if dating is a good idea for you right now at all or what drastic measures you need to take. You will hopefully be challenged at the end of each chapter as to what a good answer might be and then reflect on your answers.

As I introduce these questions to you, remember the ground rules I asked of you earlier. These questions serve as a tool as you prepare for a relationship or evaluate the one you are in. Buckle your chin strap, since this might be a bumpy ride as you search the depths of your heart. I truly hope these three questions are as helpful for you as they were for me.

Getting Personal

I remember when I met Brittany. A mutual friend named Hannah briefly introduced us, and I remember thinking, "Wow, she's gorgeous." A few months later, I ran into Hannah and Brittany at a local Starbucks we frequented. I said "Hi" and went about my business as usual, but quickly my Monday night Starbucks run became a routine in which I looked forward to running into Brittany. The more I became friends with her, the more I liked her. I often sat with her, and we both did our "work" and chatted about life.

I innocently talked Brittany into becoming a student ministry leader with us, and from then on, I was around her multiple times a week. I even had a conversation with my roommates, telling them I could no longer go to Starbucks alone because I really liked this girl and did not want to lead her on. Leading her on was in no way honoring to Christ and in every way an effort to satisfy my own desires.

In the middle of sorting through my thoughts and feelings about Brittany, my mentor Joe dropped some horrific news that changed both our lives forever. He told me he was leaving Denton and would no longer be my boss. He was moving to another state to pursue ministry there. I am not a crier, but I cried that day outside his house in his green single-cab Ford Ranger. Joe gave me confidence in life. He taught me everything I knew about ministry. My mentor, my boss, my friend was leaving.

I was bombarded with thoughts of uncertainty: *What will I do? Should I leave, or should I stay?* It was one of the most difficult times of my life. While I battled through these thoughts, the first of the three questions entered my mind. For many of you reading this book, this question might never have crossed your mind. I had never thought about it before. All this time was I wanting to date Brittany because I just needed a shoulder to cry on? Was I looking for someone to boost my confidence in Joe's absence? Why did I want to date her, after all?

The First Question

The question that popped into my head that day, the first question of the Three Question Gauntlet, is one I want you to consider with me:

Why do I want to date?
or
Why am I dating? (For those already in a relationship)

As you start down this path, be sure to approach this question objectively without tying your answers to a specific person. The question is not, "Why do I want to be in a relationship with Brian?" Do not attach a name to this question.

This is a simple question we seem to rarely or never ask. I think back to those childish relationships I was in during those early years. Your story might be just like mine. You saw a girl or guy you liked, and you got your most trusted friend from your crew to go to his or her most trusted friend to let them know you liked that person. Then the message was relayed to the potential boyfriend or girlfriend. Once they heard about it, they went back through the same chain of events to let you know they liked you too, and *voila!* You were in love!

So you went up to the girl and asked her out, using that awkward sentence you already rehearsed a hundred times. She said "yes," and now life is completely different for the both of you. You write each other's names on your book covers in nice bubble letters, sit together at the lunch table, text at odd hours of the night with little flirty emoticons, all the while hoping to make it to the level of falling asleep on the phone together—how cute.

You know what you never asked yourself? You never asked yourself why in the heck you wanted to be in a relationship in the first place. All you did was figure out someone liked you, and you just went for it. Doesn't that sound a little crazy to you? I know this because this was me, too. I never thought to ask—I just went for it.

Just as we jump into relationships without taking the time to consider the motivation, the Jews—God's chosen people introduced in the Old Testament—also often forgot to look at motivation when it came to examining their hearts as to why they were making certain choices.

In Ezra 1:1-4, a king named Cyrus issues an edict allowing the Jews to return from Babylon, where they have been held captive, to Jerusalem to rebuild the city and temple. The altar is repaired, and the foundation of the temple probably begins sometime in 537 BC. Samaritan opposition brings construction to a halt in 536 BC. Ezra 4:24 notes, "Then the work on the house of God that is in Jerusalem stopped, and it ceased until the second year of the reign of Darius king of Persia." The temple project languishes for sixteen years, until 520 BC. The temple is finally rebuilt around 516 BC.[1]

The temple was a crucial part of Jewish life. This was the place where priests offered sacrifices as a shadow of the ultimate sacrifice to come. This was the residing place for the ark of the covenant, which contained Moses' staff, manna, and the Ten Commandments. On the top of the ark was the mercy seat, where the priest spread the blood of the sacrifice and symbolically God looked down on the law inside the ark and saw it through the blood-atoning

---

[1] S. Michael Houdmann, GotQuestions.org

sacrifice that offered forgiveness of sins. This was the Jews' most holy place, where God met them, and it represented their relationship with Him. This was the dwelling place of the Almighty God.

A prophet named Haggai comes along to rebuke the people for stopping the reconstruction of the temple, and he does it by challenging their motives. Read these words of Haggai and circle the phrase you see the Lord repeats twice in Haggai 1:1–7:

> *The word of the Lord came by the hand of Haggai the prophet: "Thus says the Lord of hosts: These people say the time has not yet come to rebuild the house of the Lord." Then the word of the Lord came by the hand of Haggai the prophet, "Is it a time for you yourselves to dwell in your paneled houses, while this house lies in ruins? Now, therefore, thus says the Lord of hosts: Consider your ways. You have sown much, and harvested little. You eat, but you never have enough; you drink, but you never have your fill. You clothe yourselves, but no one is warm. And he who earns wages does so to put them into a bag with holes. Thus says the Lord of hosts: Consider your ways."*

The people decide it is not time to rebuild the temple. However they do feel it is time to panel their own homes. Homes are luxurious items, which these people prioritize over God's temple. So the Lord asks them twice to "consider your ways." He's asking them to search within their own hearts and look to what is motivating them to panel their own homes but not rebuild His. The people are putting their own wants above what the Lord wants. They are being so narrow-minded that they probably justify to themselves why they "should not" rebuild God's house but "should" focus on their own.

When it comes to relationships it is important to also consider our ways and look to what is motivating us to get into that relationship in the first place.

In Matthew 5:21–22, the author writes that Jesus said this during His famed Sermon on the Mount:

> *You have heard that it was said to those of old, "You shall not murder; and whoever murders will be liable to judgment." But I say to you that everyone who is angry with his brother will be liable to judgment; whoever insults his brother will be liable to the council; and whoever says, "You fool!" will be liable to the hell of fire.*

What is Jesus quoting from in the first verse? (Hint: there are ten of them.)

Would you say Jesus is most concerned about an action or the heart behind an action?

Jesus continues in this chapter to show us God is concerned with our hearts, not just our actions. We sometimes get so caught up in evaluating our lives based on actions that we can turn a blind eye to the motivation question—the most important question of all.

I have a little exercise that will help determine your motivation. This exercise is extremely important to this

The First Question: The One You've Never Asked

process, and it is pretty fun to explore, too. Just for a minute, take yourself out of the equation. This exercise is neither about you personally nor your relationship, but about other people around you. Write down a few motivations you have noticed in other people for starting a relationship with someone. For example, some people want a girlfriend or boyfriend because they just want the status of dating him or her. Achieving a certain status is the motivation behind some people's desire to date. I have filled in this first example for you. There are dozens of possible motivations, so have fun with this. Be sure to save some blanks for later, as you are going to need them. Do not think too hard—just look for honest, simple motivations of why people want to be in relationship.

1. Status

2. _____

3. _____

4. _____

5. _____

6. _____

7. _____

8. _____

9. _____

10. _____

11. _____

12. _____

13. _____

14. _____

15. _____

16. _____

17. _____

18. _____

19. _____

20. _____

Doing this exercise is my favorite part of giving this talk publicly. I ask the crowd to call out reasons for dating someone, and I write them on a big white board. "Dating" is defined for this book as pursuing someone you are potentially romantically interested in by spending intentional time together for the purpose of furthering that relationship.

While I was giving this talk for an all-girls Bible class at a local Christian school, one girl gave my favorite answer of all time. This was my first time giving this talk to a small room full of only girls, so I was surprised and amused when a girl from the back called out, "I want to go on dates with guys for free food!" It was an awesome answer, and the class thought it was hilarious. Although I had never heard that one before, I have learned a few common

answers over the past few years. If you do not have them on your list, I would like you to add these:
Most Common Answers to "Why Date?":
- To feel loved
- To have someone to talk to
- An emotional crutch (a shoulder to cry on)
- Bow-chicka-wow-wow (you know what I am saying, right?)
- Bored
- The person is "hot"
- Lonely
- Fun
- Friends all have someone
- The person makes you "feel good"
- Security of having a date to "the dance"

Let's be honest. Every motivation listed has been, or has the potential to be, in your mind at some point. Go back through to read each reason you listed, but this time when you read them, insert the word "I want" or maybe "I am" in front of each reason. For example, write "*I want to feel loved,*" "*I want a prom date,*" "*I want to feel good,*" "*I am bored,*" "*I want to be known for dating the hot guy.*" What do all these reasons have in common? What or who is at the center of all these motivations? You are!

Remember the primary goal for your dating relationship is *not* marriage. The primary goal is *not* your happiness, and it is *not* even his or her happiness. You get into a relationship with a girl or boy to bring glory and honor to Jesus *in* and *through* the relationship. Nevertheless, every time I do this exercise with people, we come to the same conclusion, which is that most motivations for wanting a dating relationship revolve around "*me*"! Most want to date solely for personal benefit gained from the relationship.

Say you want to be in a relationship because you are going through a tough time and just wish you had the support of a girl or a boy who makes you feel loved. You just want a shoulder to cry on. What happens when that boy or girl no longer produces this satisfaction of helping you through your troubles? What happens when she or he gets tired of listening to your problems, or when he or she does not know what advice to give? Well, you will "not love him or her anymore," and will break up.

One of my favorite examples of this heart motivation comes from a dear student from a few years back. I regularly met with him and a few of his friends, and we often shared life and walked through challenging issues together. One day he came to breakfast grinning ear to ear, telling me he was dating a girl. Because he knew my three questions, he had all his answers ready to go so I did not bother with them this time. I simply asked him to tell me about his relationship, and he told me his humbling story.

"It was so awesome," he shared. "We were walking to our cars in the parking lot, and then she said she wanted to talk to me about some stuff going on in her life. It was so legit, man. She started telling me about some things she's going through, and she just broke down right there. We talked for about an hour, and I was able to help her through her problems, and now we're dating."

I hesitated for a minute and then went out on a limb by saying, "Awesome. You'll be broken up within six months."

He and his girl lasted eight. He was a little upset with me at the time, but I was not trying to be mean. I just saw what I have seen a hundred times over. This girl was motivated by the desire to have a shoulder to cry on. She needed an emotional crutch. For him, it was probably the feeling of being needed or a sense of acceptance. I knew that sooner or later this girl would no longer need his shoulder, or at some point he would "fail" her and she would dump him. That is exactly what happened.

Although I knew his relationship would not last much past six months, I understood why he chose to date her because I have been there. Sitting outside Joe's house after hearing he was leaving the church, I wondered if I just wanted to date Brittany so I, too, had a shoulder to cry on. Was I looking for her to satisfy an emotional gap in my life? I had no idea.

Let's get more personal now. This is going to take some major brain power on your part. I want you to think of *your* motivation as to why you are dating or want to be dating. Take as much time as you need, days if needed, to write down a few reasons:

1. _____

2. _____

3. _____

4. _____

5. _____

So what can we say is the "right" answer? In your list above, are there any motivations you would call *good* motivations? Go back to your original list. Is there anything in that list that might be the "right" answer? Now, write below the one answer you think is a good reason to date. Make sure it is a good one.

_____

_____

What did you write? Which of those motivations is a good reason to date? Is wanting to feel loved a good reason, or is that using her or him to get what you want? What about wanting to date because you are bored? Have you now lowered this person to the equivalent of a video game or new pair of shoes? Maybe that person gives you the same exciting rush of killing zombies or a crazy day of shopping. After all they both give you the same thing you desire. If this is what you are after, pick the shoes. There will be much less emotional turmoil in the end. So as our list stands now, are there any good motivations that allow us to move on to the second question? Let me show you why these motivations are inadequate.

There is a disclaimer here: If you are not a God-fearing person, you might think it is OK to date a guy or girl to satisfy selfish desires. Maybe you think that honoring Christ is not a goal of yours at all. I would say to you, "Good luck, I have been there." I just want to tell you that you need to prepare yourself for disappointment and years of regret as a result of using another human being for selfish desires. You will become skilled at manipulation and suppressing the truth of your feelings and actions. The reason I know is because I, too, was once this way. I did not trust in Jesus until I was seventeen years old. At that point in my life, God invaded my heart and redeemed all that I was to make me look more like His Son. This was when I realized there is more to life than chasing a girl for fulfillment. In Christ I found the fulfillment, worth, and significance for which my heart longed. If you are looking for these elements in a fallen human, I invite you to find them in the risen King Jesus.

Going Deeper

It is an identity issue

Go back to your list and circle anything related to status. This includes "he's hot," "security of a date," "my friends have someone," and so on. If you can honestly search your heart and see you are motivated to be in a relationship with a guy or girl because of any of these reasons, I would say you are searching for identity. Often we look for identity in sports, grades, music, employment, money, living situations, and other things we do or have.

In this case you might be looking for your identity in a guy or girl. There is a major problem with this—that guy or girl will fail you. You can only find your true identity in the person of Jesus Christ. By dating this guy or girl to mark your identity, you only further lose yourself. You lose yourself when you conform to the image of who you think another person or the world wants you to be, instead of being true to the image of God. You lose your own desires, convictions, and maybe even morals to maintain an identity that is not God-centered. You slowly lose your own identity in an effort to maintain an identity as a couple. Instead of losing yourself in a guy or girl, I urge you to check out these verses in Colossians 1:21–22:

And you, who once were alienated and hostile in mind, doing evil deeds, he has now reconciled in his body of flesh by his death, in order to present you holy and blameless and above reproach before him.

This is your true identity, what it means to be identified in Christ. Using the following image, write out on the left side the three things you once were (as stated in verse 21, above). Think about those days before you knew Christ as Savior, or maybe those days do not exist for you yet because you still do not know Him as Savior. Perhaps you relate to being defined by the following three things:

1) alienated, 2) hostile, and 3) evil. I sure can—that was me for seventeen years.

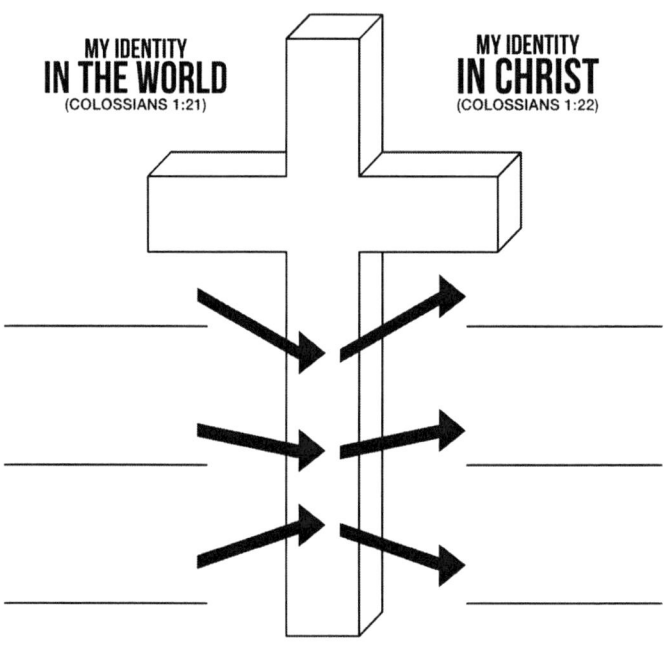

1) First, without Christ it says we are alienated. This is my identity without Christ in my life—I am alienated or isolated from God. A creepy, foreign being that is not part of the human race is called an "alien," and this is their identity. Without Christ we are alien to God and isolated from Him, and this is our identity.
2) Second, without Christ we are hostile in mind. This is a mind bitterly opposed toward the sovereign King of the universe. We are hostile in mind because this is how we are naturally bent outside of God's grace. My natural disposition defines me as alienated from God and hostile in mind toward God.
3) Third, without Christ I am defined by doing evil deeds. Have you ever wondered why people do evil deeds? While there is not just one reason, it helps to think about your younger days. Why did you bully that kid on the playground? Why did you smoke your first cigarette? Why did you gossip about some girl? Why did you pursue the party life? Why did you do some of the evil you did? Was some of it in search of an identity? Think about it. If you could be the cool kid, the popular college guy, the feared bully, the rich college graduate, the brilliant businessperson, then you would have an "identity." Being alienated from God, hostile in mind toward God, and doing evil deeds against God defined us all because we were searching for identity! If you have ever felt the evil deeds you pursued left you empty, you are not alone. So what makes you think you can find true identity doing something you were not created to do? Do not worry—there is hope.

If I am alienated from God, hostile in mind toward God, and doing evil deeds against God, this means only one thing: I rightfully receive the wrath of God against me. The wrath of God is poured out against all unrighteousness, deserved by those who are alienated from God. If these things identify me, then I have no choice but to consider myself an object of God's wrath.

So where is hope in this? Going back to the diagram, write down what God has now done (found at the beginning of verse 22 of Colossians 1) in the blank space above the cross. This is amazing! He has *reconciled* you. He restored a relationship between you and Him by becoming the very thing that would separate you from Him—sin.

On the cross Jesus reconciled you and me by absorbing the wrath of God and taking on the sins of the world. In exchange for sin, He gave us His perfect righteousness. This is Christianity! This is the changing of identity—from alienated, hostile, evil beings to perfectly restored beings. Notice in the verse that because of this reconciliation, he now presents us in a certain way. To the right of the cross, write three characteristics that describe how he presents you:

1) *Holy.* He presents you as holy. To be holy means you are set apart—namely, you are set apart for God. Notice the contrast between verse 21 and verse 22 of Colossians 1. You were once identified in the world by being alienated from God, but now because of Christ, you are presented as set apart for God—or holy.

2) *Blameless.* He presents you as blameless. Before Christ you were hostile in mind toward God, but now you are blameless before God. Before Christ you lived in the guilt of your sin or the hardening of your heart toward it. Now God takes away guilt and forgives all sin. You were seen before as guilty

for your hostility, but now Jesus declares you as not guilty.
3) *Above reproach.* He presents you as above reproach. This means no criticism can be made of you. Why? Because you now have intercession in the person of Jesus, who represents you as above reproach before the Father because of His righteousness given to you. You were doing evil deeds against God, and now you are above reproach before God!

Romans 8:33–34 tells us this:

Who shall bring any charge against God's elect? It is God who justifies. Who is to condemn? Christ Jesus is the one who died—more than that, who was raised—who is at the right hand of God, who indeed is interceding for us.

This means God is making you look less like the old you and more like His Son. This means the Holy Spirit is inside of you, tugging on your heart to put to death the deeds of the flesh and live through Him.

Because of Christ your identity has changed. Your identity in Christ is that you are holy, blameless, and above reproach. You once were alienated from God, but now you are set apart for Him. Once you were hostile in mind toward God, and now you are blameless before Him. Once you were doing evil deeds against God, and now you are above reproach in His sight.

If you date in hopes a guy or girl will give you an identity, do you think that will really last? You will slowly fool yourself into thinking you are gaining identity, but when you lose him or her, your identity gets lost with it. My point is that no guy or girl can ever give you your true identity—only Jesus can.

It is a love issue

Flip back a few pages and draw a box around any answers related to your emotions. For example, box in "a shoulder to cry on," "an emotional crutch," "to feel loved," "someone to talk to," or "loneliness." If any of these are motivations of why you want to be in a relationship, you might be looking for a lost love.

Maybe as a girl you never felt loved by your dad and so search out some chivalrous guy to fill that void. Maybe you never had a loving home and are searching for that feeling you hear others talking about. Possibly there was abuse, and you are unwittingly looking to a guy or girl to heal that. It could be you grew up in a very loving home and saw incredible parents live out an incredible marriage so you would do anything to have that yourself.

We all have a great desire to be loved, and being loved is a good thing. However, sometimes we can manipulate people, lie to ourselves, and do crazy things just to be loved. We watch TV shows that sometimes portray unrealistic expectations of being loved, and we would do anything to feel what they seem to feel or at least what they communicate that they feel. Because there are endless possibilities to this question, the thing on the table that must be addressed is this: Are you looking for a lost love to be filled by a boyfriend or girlfriend?

In 1 John 4:7–10, we get a look into what love really is. In this exercise underline each time you see the word "love."

> *Beloved, let us love one another, for love is from God, and whoever loves has been born of God and knows God. Anyone who does not love does not know God, because God is love.*

In this the love of God was made manifest among us, that God sent his only Son into the world, so that we might live through him. In this is love, not that we have loved God but that he loved us and sent his Son to be the propitiation for our sins.

In the blanks provided below, complete these statements found in the above passage about love:

We are to love _____ _____.

Love is _____ _____.

Whoever loves has been _____ _____ _____.

Whoever loves _____ _____.

Whoever does not love _____ _____ _____ _____.

God is _____.

God's love was made manifest by His _____.

God showed love by sending _____ _____.

Complete this sentence in your own words: *After reading the passage in 1 John 4, I know I'm loved because…*

_____

_____

Love is that God satisfied His wrath, or propitiation, in His own Son at a time when you and I were enemies to Him. At a time when we were alienated from Him, hostile toward Him, and doing evil deeds against Him, He loved us anyway! This is love that no matter how bad, messed up, dysfunctional, irreparable, or disgusting we acted, God made a way for us to experience His love!

He is love, He created love, and He is the standard of love. Also notice that outside of Him, we truly do not know what love is. You want to feel loved? Go to the one who created love. You want a shoulder to cry on? Go to the one who experienced death, pain, and tears just like you do. You want someone to talk to? Talk to the one who knows your thoughts before you can even speak them and loves you just the same.

Jesus says to us in Matthew 11:28, "Come to me, all who labor and are heavy laden, and I will give you rest. Take my yoke upon you, and learn from me, for I am gentle and lowly in heart, and you will find rest for your souls."

If you are looking for some girl or guy to satisfy this perceived absence of love in your heart or fill an unrealistic expectation set by Hollywood, then you will be disappointed. You will end up using this girl or guy as an emotional syringe as you pump a false sense of love and belonging into your veins. This in no way is honoring to Christ and is a ticking time bomb to a bad ending when that person no longer satisfies your craving for love.

It is a purpose issue

For this last example, go back and underline any motivations that have to do with being bored, having fun, physical pleasure, and such. At this point most of your answers should be marked with a circle, box, or line. As you look at the answers you just underlined and examine your own motivation to date, you might think some of the reasons you want to date are harmless—and you could be right.

However, if you are looking for a relationship to put some fun and excitement in your life, I am not sure you will get what you are actually here for. If you think this relationship gives you purpose, you are mistaken. You are not only mistaken, but you also are missing out on living life to the fullest. The relationship is not the purpose you were made for—it is only a way for you to accomplish your divine purpose. Let me take a few minutes to show you exactly what you are missing. Read through Genesis 1:26–27:

> *Then God said, "Let us make man in our image, after our likeness."...So God created man in his own image, in the image of God he created him; male and female he created them.*

Write down some observations:
What are the words most repeated in the above text?

_____

_____

What is the main idea of this text in Genesis?

_____

_____

How did God decide to make or create man?

_____

_____

This text in Genesis 1 has some major weight if we see it for what it really is. God specifically says He has created us to bear His image and be in His likeness. This means we are to be image bearers of the King of the universe, God Himself. To bear someone's image means you are his or her representation. You are an ambassador. To bear God's image means we represent Him in many ways. We do this through love, relationship, and righteousness, among many other godly attributes.

Adam was the first man created, and he was meant to magnify and glorify the name of the King. You and I were originally created to bear this image of the King, to display His righteousness, mercy, love, grace, and all that He is. However, because of sin, we no longer are able to bear this image of the eternal King. This is where the gospel comes in. It restores us to a place where we can once again bear the image of the King through Jesus' righteousness. If you are not doing what you were created to do, then of course you will look for some other purpose in life, and that other purpose will leave you empty.

Read through this text in Colossians 1:16, and make a few observations:

> *For by him all things were created, in heaven and on earth, visible and invisible, whether thrones or dominions or rulers or authorities—all things were created through him and for him.*

Is there anything He did not create?

_____

_____

Why did He create all things?

_____

_____

    This text simply states that all things were created for God. This means *you* were created by God and for God. Period.

    Now observe this passage in Ephesians 2:10, and make some notes about what you read:

For we are his workmanship, created in Christ Jesus for good works, which God prepared beforehand, that we should walk in them.

Some translations use the word "masterpiece" in place of "workmanship." In your own words, describe what a masterpiece is:

_____

_____

_____

What are you created for?

_____

_____

_____

So who or what is at the pinnacle, or top, of all God's creation?

_____

_____

Why?

_____

_____

Let me give you a different example. Let's say you are created to be an Xbox controller. Your lot in life is to be used by a player to represent his wishes through the console. When you allow the user to place you in his or her hands, you are at your best. However, if you were to look across the room at the alarm clock and wish you could tell time and make annoying sounds to wake people up, you would be in for a world of disappointment. You can try all you want, but you cannot tell time. If you try to tell time and function as an alarm clock, you will look like an idiot. This is often how we approach and interact with God. We are created to be used by God to display His image to the world. When we fail to do that, we look as stupid as an Xbox controller trying to be an alarm clock. It leaves us empty inside.

This is what happens to some of us when we have no greater purpose in life. We are a masterpiece of God's creation, created to bear His image, but if we lose sight of this, we lose purpose. We might try to find this purpose in being the perfect boyfriend or girlfriend, but all the while we are an Xbox controller trying to function as an alarm clock. Your issue has nothing to do with the relationship and everything to do with Jesus.

All of these issues of identity, love, and purpose have the same answer—Jesus. If the relationship you are currently in is motivated by any of the reasons listed above, stop where you are, put your relationship on hold, and get raw with Jesus. First seek Christ. Although answering the question, "But why?" seems tough, it is easier than you think. It is difficult to admit the truth but easy to find the solution. The solution is that your identity is found in Christ. You are fully loved in Christ. You have a greater purpose than anything imaginable through the person of Christ, who has restored you to be an image bearer of the King.

A Good Answer

Remember our original question:
Why do I want to date?
Or
Why am I dating?

Take a second and flip back to your lists of *why* you want to date. Over the many times I have gone through this with people, I find one common theme over and over. Do you remember it? The common theme in all your answers is probably *you*. We tend to view life through a selfish lens that puts us at the center of the universe. We all desire to be satisfied, happy, fulfilled, and whatever else might make us feel better in the moment.

I believe there is an answer that satisfies the first question and allows you to move onto the second stage of the Three Question Gauntlet. Keep in mind that we have already determined God and His glory as the goal, so what is one answer that can be considered "good" and selfless? It is a simple answer.

Question: *Why do I want to date? (or why am I dating?)*
Answer: *Because of her or him!*

Yes, at first glance this seems to be a very self-centered answer and even contradictory to what I have already said. However, it actually proves to be the opposite. The answer is, *I want to be in a relationship because of who this person is—not because of what I want.* This answer forces us to put our own selfish motivations aside and see her or him for who they really are. It also allows us to put aside our own desires and consider the Lord's desires in this situation. We get to more objectively view the relationship and remove the selfish nature within us all.

You need to want to date that girl or guy for *who he or she is in Christ*, not for what the person does, not for what the person can give you, not for a lost love, not for a purpose, and not for any motivation listed. To truly say this, first remove the tendency to view relationships with "self" as the center. I believe this is a great first step in achieving the goal of honoring Christ both *in* and *through* the relationship. If we are at the center of our universe, or in this case our dating relationship, we can never live fully for God's glory. It is difficult to put Christ on his rightful throne while it is being occupied by this guy or girl.

Can you honestly say you are simply motivated to date a guy or girl because of the person he or she is? If you are on the verge of entering into a dating relationship, can you honestly say it is because of who that person is? Most of the time, we are motivated by what we think that person can give us, instead of who that person is.

Getting Personal

Sitting outside my boss and friend Joe's house that day after learning of his departure, I was confused. I did not trust myself. I wondered if maybe all those nights at Starbucks with Brittany were some sort of cheap counseling session to help me through this time in my life.

Maybe I had a hidden motivation of wanting a girl to talk to in my time of need.

Joe moved shortly thereafter, but my conversations with him about Brittany continued. Each week I called to fill him in with the most recent updates, and he challenged me on my journey. Finally after about six months of prayer, I called Joe for our weekly conversation.

"Joe, I just don't know if I should date her. I am praying that God will have her date someone else if He does not want this thing to happen. I just need to pray a little more," I said.

"How long have you been praying about this?" Joe cunningly asked.

"Oh, about six months," I replied.

"And what makes you think God hasn't heard you over these past six months?" he answered.

That day I realized that maybe, just maybe, I actually liked this girl just for who she is. I decided that day I wanted to date because I genuinely liked Brittany as a person. I saw Christ in her, or better yet, I saw her hidden in Christ.

Reflection Questions on *Why do I want to be in a dating relationship?*

What would you say your motivation for dating was before you read this chapter?

_____

_____

_____

_____

Has that motivation changed?

_____

_____

_____

If you wrote "yes" to the above question, why has it changed? Explain.

_____

_____

_____

_____

THE SECOND QUESTION: PROVE IT

During those months when I was debating whether or not to ask Brittany out on a date, I wrestled through that first question: *Why do I want to date?* When I finally came to the conclusion that it was simply who Brittany was in Christ that motivated me to want to date her, I somehow still doubted myself. I doubted my answer was as genuine as it could be. Was the answer just the good "Christian" answer I knew I should give? Or was this a true reflection of my heart's motivation? I knew I could easily deceive myself at this point, so doubt still loomed in my mind.

I saw Brittany several times a week through student ministries and mutual friends. I made it a point to grow in my friendship with her and get to know her better, without leading her on. My thoughts were often bent toward her and the potential of dating her. Because of my lack of trust in my own judgment, I told myself to prove why I liked her. If I really was motivated by who she was in Christ, I should be able to back up that statement. So one day in my prayer journal, I wrote out all the things Brittany was—not what she did, but who she was. It only took a few minutes to fill up a page, and as the days went by and I continued getting to know her, I added to that list.

I will never forget one night when we both "accidentally" bumped into each other at Starbucks, and I found yet another reason to support my answer. It was around Valentine's Day, and she was student teaching at a nearby elementary school. Like any good teacher, she was writing her students those little tear-out Valentine's cards you got when you were a kid. During this time, some of the staff tasked me with keeping a weekly blog for our ministry. I did not love writing the blog, but each Monday night at Starbucks I put together a short post for the page. Brittany knew I did not love blogging and that I was working on that week's post. About that time she slid over a Valentine's card written to me, and it read, "Great job blogging!"

I knew two things at this point. One, she was at least somewhat interested in me. Two, she was sharing her gift of encouragement with me. I still have that card to this day, and my hunch was right. My wife is extremely gifted in encouragement and shares that gift often. If I had not spent the time to get to know her, I would have not known she had that gift. That was the night I realized I was truly motivated by *who she was*.

The Second Question

The first question we walked through is, *Why do I want to be in a dating relationship?* This is a general question with no name attached to it. The second question I want you to ask yourself is this:

Why do I want to be in a relationship with him or her?

This question gets specific. This is not a question to scrutinize or shift blame to the person you want to date or are dating. This question is for you. It is a question to make you prove to yourself that you have not lied your way through the first question. Or maybe you answered

The Second Question: Prove It

the first question but you just do not know enough about the other person yet. This is the question I had to ask myself in order to overcome the doubt I had in myself. As you think through this question, be careful not to let yourself give examples that describe *what he or she does*, but rather give examples that describe *who he or she is*. When Brittany gave me that Valentine's card at Starbucks that night, it was not about the feeling she gave me—rather it was a glimpse into her heart behind the action of giving me the card. She gave me the card because she was sharing her gift of encouragement with me. I saw her as an encourager, so it was not about something she did but who she was.

If I were sitting across the table from you at Chick-fil-A, and you just told me you wanted to date because of who someone is, I would be thrilled! Next I would say, "Prove it." You would look at me a little concerned and maybe even frustrated.

Whenever I talk to people about this, they often look at me with concern and frustration as well. I love keeping them on their toes. One way I like to do this is by talking down as many sports as I can. I start by saying how easy football is because all you do is run around hitting people really hard. Volleyball is child's play—any game you can play in a swimming pool is a kids' game, and you have *three tries* to get the ball over the net. And then there's baseball, which is the most boring sport on earth. If being a good player means running around and catching a little white ball, then my dog is the all-time best baseball player. How about basketball? Run, jump, dunk—easy.

Then I sarcastically talk about my sport, a man's sport, the most difficult sport—golf! Yes, golf! At this point most people are jokingly booing me. But what makes golf so amazing? Golf requires you to navigate through a set of fourteen different clubs separated by seven grams per club head or else the shafts do not work properly. The shafts must be frequencied out—have I impressed you yet with all my technical golf talk?—at a certain cycle per minute to produce the shot you desire.

You have to pick the perfect club for that one shot. Then you have to swing that club at just the right angle, just the right speed, using just the right muscles at just the right time to produce a load in the shaft as you take the club back and then get it in what's called "the slot" for the shaft to release at just the right time so the perfectly weighted club head squares up at impact. Then you must maintain an approach angle with which the club does not hit too little or too much of that small white ball.

If you somehow managed to put all this together, you'd better also hope your body alignment was right, you checked the wind before the swing, and your tempo is in perfect sync for that particular shot. I haven't even talked about other parts of the game. That is just the swing! And that is why golf is the most difficult sport in the world.

Most of the time I get laughter and applause as a light hearted response, even though few really comprehended what was said about the game of golf. The truth is, I do not really think those things about other sports. In fact basketball is probably my favorite sport, and I am a fantasy-football fanatic. My point is that if you are going to make such a bold statement like I did about golf, then you'd better be able to back it up. In the same way, if you can honestly say you want to date a guy or girl because of who he or she is, then you need to back up that statement.

Think about this for a few minutes. What is so special about that person? Are you sure it is not just the fact that he or she makes you feel good? Is it that he or she is just gorgeous so you cannot pass up this opportunity? In the space provided below, list out the characteristics that influence you to want to date the person.

The Second Question: Prove It

1. _____
2. _____
3. _____
4. _____
5. _____
6. _____
7. _____
8. _____
9. _____
10. _____
11. _____
12. _____

Now, take out your pen, and get ready to mark up the following Scripture passages. Circle every word or phrase that describes a positive attribute or attitude about someone you might want to date. I understand this context is set inside the confines of marriage. However, some godly attitudes are found in them, so read closely.

Ephesians 5:1–4
> Therefore, be imitators of God, as beloved children. And walk in love, as Christ loved us and gave himself up for us, a fragrant offering and sacrifice to God. But sexual immorality and all impurity or covetousness must not even be named among you, as is proper among saints. Let there be no filthiness nor foolish talk nor crude joking, which are out of place, but instead let there be thanksgiving.

Galatians 5:22–23
> But the fruit of the Spirit is love, joy, peace, patience, kindness, goodness, faithfulness, gentleness, self-control.

Proverbs 31:10–31
An excellent wife who can find?
   She is far more precious than jewels.
The heart of her husband trusts in her,
   and he will have no lack of gain.
She does him good, and not harm,
   all the days of her life.
She seeks wool and flax,
   and works with willing hands.
She is like the ships of the merchant;
   she brings her food from afar.
She rises while it is yet night
   and provides food for her household
   and portions for her maidens.
She considers a field and buys it;
   with the fruit of her hands she plants a vineyard.
She dresses herself with strength
   and makes her arms strong.
She perceives that her merchandise is profitable.

Her lamp does not go out at night.
She puts her hands to the distaff,
  and her hands hold the spindle.
She opens her hand to the poor
  and reaches out her hands to the needy.
She is not afraid of snow for her household,
  for all her household are clothed in scarlet.
She makes bed coverings for herself;
  her clothing is fine linen and purple.
Her husband is known in the gates
  when he sits among the elders of the land.
She makes linen garments and sells them;
  she delivers sashes to the merchant.
Strength and dignity are her clothing,
  and she laughs at the time to come.
She opens her mouth with wisdom,
  and the teaching of kindness is on her tongue.
She looks well to the ways of her household
  and does not eat the bread of idleness.
Her children rise up and call her blessed;
  her husband also, and he praises her:
"Many women have done excellently,
  but you surpass them all."
Charm is deceitful, and beauty is vain,
  but a woman who fears the Lord is to be praised.
Give her of the fruit of her hands,
  and let her works praise her in the gates.

Psalm 15:1–5
O Lord, who shall sojourn in your tent?
  Who shall dwell on your holy hill?
He who walks blamelessly and does what is right
  and speaks truth in his heart;
who does not slander with his tongue
  and does no evil to his neighbor,
  nor takes up a reproach against his friend;

> in whose eyes a vile person is despised,
>   but who honors those who fear the Lord;
> who swears to his own hurt and does not change;
> who does not put out his money at interest
>   and does not take a bribe against the innocent.
> He who does these things shall never be moved.

Below, write out the characteristics you would like in your future husband or wife (for example, "enjoys being with people," "kind," "encouraging," "values family time"). Try to make sure these are unselfish, godly traits you seek.

1. _____

2. _____

3. _____

4. _____

5. _____

6. _____

7. _____

8. _____

9. _____

10. _____

11. _____

12. _____

Finally, in the space provided below, rewrite your original list from the beginning of this chapter, plus the things you circled in the passages, plus the list you just made.

Traits you like about who he or she is:

1. _____

2. _____

3. _____

4. _____

5. _____

6. _____

7. _____

8. _____

9. _____

10. _____

11. _____

12. _____

Traits you circled in the Scripture passages:

1. _____
2. _____
3. _____
4. _____
5. _____
6. _____
7. _____
8. _____
9. _____
10. _____
11. _____
12. _____

Traits you want in a future spouse:

1. _____
2. _____
3. _____
4. _____

5. _____

6. _____

7. _____

8. _____

9. _____

10. _____

11. _____

12. _____

Do some of these overlap? Are your reasons more about *what he or she does* or *who he or she is*? Do you find your reasons are more about physical things and not heart-centered things? Maybe your reasons continue to be about you and what you get out of the deal? At the end of the day, you want to date someone who puts God ahead of even you. You can get a glimpse of this by observing just who the person is. His or her relationship with Christ, or lack thereof, determines who he or she is. Are the reasons you want to date this person good reasons after all?

Chances are you can look back at the lists to quickly discover if you are "in like" with someone or simply infatuated. For our purposes here, I chose to use the phrase "in like" in an effort to not confuse or devalue the phrase "in love." So maybe we can agree that at this point in the process someone is at least falling "in like" with another.

I was sitting at breakfast with a student one day, and he was telling me about his homecoming date options with the potential of starting a relationship with one "lucky" lady. I listened to the list fly across the table and decided I would play this up a little bit. I asked him about the three girls, and he gave me his little list in order of preference. The girl at the top was one I had never heard him or his friends talk about before, so I asked who she was. His response was classic. "Well, I do not really know her," he said.

"If you don't know her but want to date her, you must think she's hot," I said.

"Oh, ya, she's smokin' hot. All I really know about her is her reputation," he said.

"Well," I playfully continued, "what's her reputation like?"

"I mean, it is not the best. I don't know. I really don't know her," he admitted.

"So tell me about the other girls then," I pressed.

"Well, I know one of them really well. She is a really great girl. Some dude will be lucky to date her," he replied.

I started in heavy this time. "So the girl you know well, are already friends with, and respect is not the best option because she's not as hot as the other girl? Not to mention, with this other girl's reputation you might get a little something physical going on that night. So the only question I have is, why are you having this conversation with me? You know my answer."

"Ya," he laughed in response, "I just don't know what to do."

"You know exactly what to do," I said, "and I think you are having this conversation with me because you want me to make a demand on what you should do. That way you do not have to search your own heart but rather you can follow some stale rule. Not to mention, I think you are too much of a coward to make the right decision on your own." I had met with this student for years, so we had some trust built up between us that allowed me to say this to him.

I continued, "I don't even know any of these girls, but I know you shouldn't date them. The fact you do not even know your 'number-one pick', and you still want to date her tells me all I need to know. There is no way the motivation for this is God-centered. Keeping your studly status and possibly get something physical out of the deal that night is what is motivating you. Now you tell me how this is honoring to Christ, and I will tell you to go for it."

The conversation ended there. I knew he did not care about honoring Christ.

The issue with my friend, and a lot of us, is that we think we are "in love" or "in like" but are really just infatuated. Let's take a moment to make sure we fully understand the difference between the two.

Going Deeper

Love vs. Infatuation

I use the word "love" loosely here. Being "in love" with someone is often misunderstood, but this book is not to address this issue directly. Here I want to show you a difference between being "in like," or "in love," and being infatuated. I define infatuation as *a short-lived, self-centered passion for someone.* You might be infatuated with a celebrity. It is unreasonable that you would ever be in any sort of relationship with that person, but the poster hangs in your room. I am not saying this is bad—I am simply making a point.

In an effort to oversimplify at first, let's define being in love as *an affectionate commitment to each other over time.* The problem is that it is tough to tell the difference between being in love and being infatuated. I am going to give you three diagnostic statements to help you determine if you are infatuated or in love.

1. If you have options, it is probably infatuation. This means there are two or three guys or girls on your radar, and you are just deciding which of the three best suits you. If you are trying to decide between multiple people, it is probably infatuation. This is a dead giveaway that you are not in it for the other person. In fact, you are in it for yourself so much that you basically have these guys or girls going around on a conveyer belt, trying to decide which best suits you. If you have options, you have failed Question #1. However, this does not mean you are a bad person. This simply means you need to stop and realize the emotional junk you are about to put yourself and those people through and the almost guaranteed failure of a relationship. From the get-go, it is all about you.

2. If your thoughts are consumed with him or her, it is probably infatuation. If you find yourself taking screenshots of his or her Facebook profile just to put in your camera roll, you are probably consumed. If you have memorized his or her class schedule, practice times, dinner times, and favorite deodorant, you are probably consumed. By being consumed with another human, you are on your way to making an idol. Be consumed with the person of Jesus Christ, who is not held by even death, over a finite human. Be consumed with God in your life, not which guy or girl you hope comes into your life. Being consumed with someone other than Christ means you are placing your hope and your joy in that person. Would you rather place this hope in a finite being or in the infinite Creator who loves you more than you can ever imagine? Take this infatuation to the Lord, and give it to Him. Tear down this idol in your life before God lovingly rips it out for you.

3. If you think your world would come to an end if you were to break up or did not end up dating, it is probably infatuation. If you honestly think you "could not live without him or her," it is probably infatuation. If you stay up at night reading into every text message or cannot sleep until he or she calls to say good night, it is probably infatuation. This is a relationship built around fear—fear that you will lose the person, that you are not adequate, and that God doesn't control the relationship but you do. It is one that is controlled only by manipulation. If you are in this situation, get out! Live in the freedom of who Christ has made you to be.

If you are in a relationship or interested in a relationship because of infatuation, you might think it is no big deal. But remember your goal. If your goal is to make yourself feel good or look good, congratulations—you are on your way...at least for a little while. But if your goal is to honor Christ both *in* and *through* this relationship, then how is infatuation honoring to him? I say this type of relationship is not honoring to Christ but honoring to you. It is very likely that if you get into a relationship because of infatuation, it will end in regret. The heart behind these types of relationships produces jealousy and insecurity. Infatuations leave you envious about other guys or girls the other talks to, anxious about why he or she has not called, and constantly wondering if he or she still "loves" you. The bottom line is that infatuation with temporal things leaves you empty, depressed, and regretful. Being in love with someone—which I am not saying happens right away—can end in a secure, confident relationship.

Take a moment to explore what the Apostle Paul has to say about love...

1 Corinthians 13:4–7

Love is patient and kind; love does not envy or boast; it is not arrogant or rude. It does not insist on its own way; it is not irritable or resentful; it does not rejoice at wrongdoing, but rejoices with the truth. Love bears all things, believes all things, hopes all things, endures all things.

List out what love is:

P_____

K_____

Does not E_____

Does not B_____

Is not A_____

Is not R_____

Does not I_____

Is not I_____

Is not R_____

Does not at W_____

But rejoices with T_____

Love B_____ B_____

H_____ and

E_____ all things

In the space below, briefly write three different times you have experienced any of the specific parts of being loved that are mentioned in 1 Corinthians 13:4-7. For example, you might write by number 1, "Patient—my teacher with my bad grades."

1. _____

_____

2. _____

_____

3. _____

_____

It is important to understand a biblical basis of love. Love contains feelings, but it is not a feeling. Love is exciting, but love is not based on excitement. Love creates emotions, but it does not spring from an emotion. Please consider the difference in acting lovingly toward someone and claiming to be in love with someone. In keeping with my efforts to not write tons of Christian dating advice, I'll let you and the Spirit wrestle through that one. Enjoy.

Trouble Drafting the List?

Read back through the lists you made on pages 81-87. If you are currently in a relationship and are having trouble making these lists about your girlfriend or boyfriend, I am going to just go out on a limb and say you are in trouble. The reason I say this is because if you do not even know who the person is, there is no way you are in that relationship for anything other than yourself. Selfish relationships are destructive relationships.

On the other hand, maybe you have someone on your radar you want to date but do not yet know enough about him or her. Perhaps you are barely even friends at this point. If this is you, my suggestion is to enjoy spending time getting to know the person as a friend. After all, why would you want to date someone you are not even friends with first? There is nothing wrong with finding ways to be in groups around this person or to have conversations to get to know him or her.

Still, there are some poor choices you could make in simply getting to know someone as friends. If you say you are just friends with someone but you treat the person like a boyfriend or girlfriend, then you are not really just friends. For example, if you text this person on a daily basis, show up at volleyball games, or find yourself "dropping by" his or her house late at night, then you are really a dating couple merely labeling yourselves "friends."

If you set up a weekly "hey, let's get breakfast as friends, and I will pick you up and pay" and say you are just friends, I strongly disagree. If this is you, then you are going about this the "wrong" way. You are communicating one set of expectations while living out another. This forces you to manipulate yourself and the other person in an effort to maintain the relationship.

I want to introduce a tool that might be helpful in searching your heart. This tool specifically deals with communication and expectation. I call it "dating in windows."

Dating in Windows

One of my favorite words I've heard used is the word "frating." This is the person who says they are just friends but in every practical way is actually dating. This method of relationship is appealing to some because it seems to come with all the worldly benefits of dating with none of the commitment and dating problems. The issue with this is that it gets confusing really fast. I'm sure this is why, back in the day, Facebook invented this relationship status: "It's complicated." Another way you can help clarify your motivation and double-check your list is to see if you are "dating in windows."

When Brittany and I remodeled our house, we decided to put in a large window that looks into the backyard from the living room. I cannot tell you how many times in a week I sit in our living room and look out that window. It looks out into a heavily wooded backyard, where our crazy cat chases lizards and anything else that moves. The problem with our house is that it is arranged in such a way that you cannot see the pool from the back window. We have this huge window I look out of every day, but I can never see the pool from that window. Sometimes it is a bummer, but I have a certain expectation of what I will see when I look out that window. If I want to see the pool, I have to go to a different part of the house and look out a different window. It would be foolish for me to sit in my living room and expect to see the pool.

Relationships are similar to the windows in my house. If you are looking out of a certain relationship "window," certain expectations are tied to that window. Every relationship you have has a set of expectations on it. You have acquaintances you are in relationship with, and you have a limited view of that relationship. Your view from the perspective of an acquaintance is that you probably do not have a phone number, but you are friends on social media. You might not talk much except when you randomly run into each other with mutual friends.

If you were to change "windows" and view that acquaintance as a friend, your expectations would change. As friends it is normal to call, text, and hang out with them.

You no longer have the same view you once had, and you have changed your view by redefining your relationship. Of course you do not have a formal conversation about this—it simply happens naturally. The more time you spend around a person, the more likely you are to develop a closer relationship. Each relationship naturally evolves into a different stage, or window, as time goes on. If it does not evolve into the next stage, the relationship is usually over in guy/girl dating relationships.

For the sake of this book, let's break the stages of relationships into the following windows:

Acquaintances. This is a person you know only in passing. You might be social-media friends, but you probably do not even have a phone number.

Friends. This is a person you have known for a little while and have spent some quality time with. You probably have a number in your phone and hang out with this person and other friends on a frequent basis.

Dating. This is a person you have intentionally pursued in starting a relationship. You go out with him or her alone, in an effort to just spend time, have fun, and to get to know each other better.

Social Media Official. I think it is a funny term and defines this stage well. This is when you have been dating awhile, and you both decide it is getting "serious." You have an awkward conversation about whether or not you should call each other "boyfriend" and "girlfriend," and you take your relationship to the next level and go public with it!

Engagement. This is where you just cannot stand dating anymore, and you decide you have to marry this person. Through much prayer and counsel, this is the stage in which you are ready to pop the question.

Marriage. This is the stage when all aspects of life are shared with each other. This is a holy union, a promise, created by God to represent Christ to the church.

Let's place each of the stages into a window below:

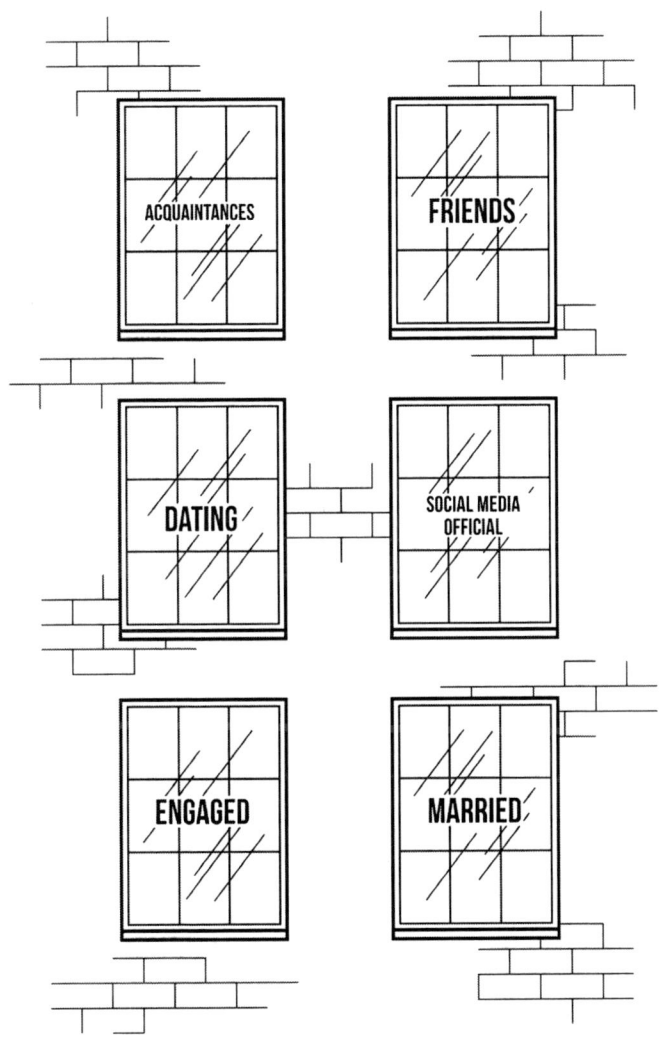

Now comes the fun part. With your pen, mark an X in the window you are currently in with the guy or girl you are pursuing or thinking of pursuing. After you have made your X, list below some normal expectations for that current window. For example, if you were to mark "Friends," you might write, "treat like any other friend," "group interaction," "no regular texts or calls," "no one-on-one dates," "no favoritism." Those are just a few that pop into my head. Take your time to list out any expectations you think are normal for the window you are currently in.

1. _____
2. _____
3. _____
4. _____
5. _____
6. _____
7. _____
8. _____
9. _____
10. _____

A student I was close with years ago liked a certain girl. She went to a different school, but he met her through mutual friends. He got her phone number a few days after meeting her and began texting her every day. About two

The Second Question: Prove It

weeks later, he bought her a single rose of her favorite color and surprised her by placing it on her car after school with a note. She melted when she saw the rose. Of course they were just friends (they said). As I talked with him about this girl, it was plain this was a classic case of defining yourself in one window and actually living in another.

The problem is that in the girl's mind, she thought they were practically dating. Her friends asked if they were dating, and she usually responded with "I'm not sure" or "not yet." This guy thought he was being a gentleman, but he was being a manipulator who was leading on a girl. It was not about her at all—it was about the pursuit.

After months of leading her on, they eventually called it what it was—dating. Soon after that, the guy lost interest and so began to pursue her physically. That kept his attention awhile, but soon he lost interest in that, too, and dumped her. Then he ran back to me, and guess what he said? No, he did not say, "You were right," or, "I really messed up with her."

He simply said, "Dude, I really have been running from God. I feel so far from Him. Will you help me?"

This is the danger of defining your relationship in one window and living in another. If you have been dating awhile and are planning a life together, where you will live, what jobs you will have, how many kids you want, and things of that nature, fellas, you'd better be ring shopping at the same time. To put those expectations on the relationship while only dating is destructive and hurtful. Do not treat a friend as a boyfriend or girlfriend and just call yourself "friends." Either ask her out, just be friends, or cut ties. Girls, if a guy is calling you his friend and treating you like his girlfriend, call him out or cut ties.

In fairness, there is a level at which this has to happen for a short amount of time. You have probably heard people talk about DTR (defining the relationship). This is what they are talking about. If you find yourself moving from one window to the next, it is time for a DTR (define the relationship). This is when you clearly communicate how you feel, where the relationship is, and what you expect. I understand this conversation might be awkward at first, but it's not nearly as awkward as it will be if you do not have it. The question you must ask yourself is this: *Is my passiveness in not having a DTR honoring Christ?*

Look back to your list about expectations that go along with the window you are currently in. Are you holding to those expectations? Are you leading him or her on? If you live outside of those expectations, you need to put on the brakes and back up, or take the relationship to the next window. Are you ready to do that? How do you even *know* if you are ready to do that? Hold that thought until we get to the third question.

Red Flags

Another way we can help clarify motivation and double-check the lists is to become aware of red flags. In any relationship, there are potential red flags. These red flags make it obvious you should not be in that relationship or there are some drastic changes you need to make. Most of these red flags, however, have more to do with you and your heart than with the other person. In other words, if you see red flags in yourself or in someone else, it is a good indication you should not be dating. Though you may be tempted to ignore red flags or lie to yourself about them so you can carry out some poorly motivated reason to start dating, please consider these red flags in your own dating relationship or desire to date.

Red Flag: Pressuring you to do what you do not want to do

While this pressure could come from anywhere, the most obvious form of pressure is found in the physical aspects of the relationship. Again my goal here is not to spell out these specifics. Guys and girls, if the person you are dating constantly pressures you to do things you are not comfortable with, this is a huge red flag! Reevaluate where you have lied to yourself, and get out quick. To be in a relationship means you are out for the other person's best interest, so your boyfriend or girlfriend should be constantly looking (not always succeeding) to serve you and not self. Also, look past the physical, even though this is the place it is easiest to spot, as there are many other areas in which you might feel pressured.

Another area could be emotional pressure, such as when someone manipulates another to feed emotional desire. This is most commonly done through texting or messaging on the computer. In these cases someone is setting you up to feed an emotional hole in his or her heart. I have even seen multiple times when so much emotional pressure is put on the other person that suicide is threatened if the other person does not come through.

We should consider setting boundaries because of what God tells us in 1 Peter 1:16:

> But as he who called you is holy, you also be
> holy in all your conduct, since it is written,
> "You shall be holy, for I am holy."

To be holy means we are set apart, more specifically "set apart unto God, for God." This means as Christians we are to be what the Bible calls "above reproach," to "walk in a manner worthy of God." Your Christ-centered relationship should be different than the world's standard of what a relationship looks like.

Red Flag: He or she has unstable friendships
In my opinion, good dating relationships start with good friendships. If the person you like constantly gossips about friends, he or she is probably not someone you want to date. If they are always changing friend groups because of bickering, then you are probably dealing with an insecure person you do not want to date. If the person seems to always stab friends in the back or is untrustworthy to best friends, you probably do not want to date this person. If the person cannot even be friends with those closest with him or her, what makes you think the person will make a good boyfriend or girlfriend? Go back through your motivations discussed in regard to question number two—*Why do I want to be in a relationship with him or her?*—and see where you have lied to yourself.

Red Flag: You are unsure if he or she is a follower of Christ
If you cannot answer this question, the red flag here could be one of two things: 1) You do not know the person well enough yet and should give it some time. 2) You know the person is not a follower of Christ, but you are trying to justify it to yourself to feel good about dating him or her. This is a crucial aspect to the journey of your relationship. If you are a follower of Christ and the other person is not, you immediately set yourself up for a difficult time. For a believer to date an unbeliever is unwise, for a believer to marry an unbeliever is unbiblical (2 Corinthians 6:14).

As you think about this red flag, be careful not to view people's relationship with Christ by thinking about what they *do* but about who they *are*. I cannot tell you how many times I have asked this question to our students about someone they like and have received the same misguided answer. Many students usually respond with what church a potential boyfriend or girlfriend attends, or they relay the information that a crush sometimes attends student ministries. I do not ask if potential dates go to church—I am asking about their relationship with Christ. See the difference?

Red Flag: Morally you two do not see eye to eye as God sees fit

This is tied into that last flag about both being Christ followers, but it is a little more specific. This difference in morals can set you up for failure. A difference in morals really stems from your own worldview. If you both do not have similar morals or convictions, trouble is brewin'.

Here is a small example of what I mean. One of you thinks it's okay to cuss, and the other does not. Should that person just not cuss around you? Should he put on a show for you and not reveal to you who he really is? Or are you going to stop cussing "for him or her," and then start back up all over again when you break up? If this is the situation you find yourself in, take heed of this red flag.

Here is an example that could deeply hurt your relationship in the future. Say one of you thinks church is something you should both be committed to, but the other does not. One of you goes while the other sleeps in, and this goes on for years. Later in life you get engaged, and then you get married and have children, still following this same regimen of church. When the kids get old enough, where do they go? Do they respect the one who sleeps in or look down at him or her? Maybe you are a product of this, and you understand all too well. Yes, it is possible for God to redeem this situation. However, it is also possible to leave your family in great confusion.

Red Flag: You avoid godly advice

If you find yourself navigating these waters without the counsel of older godly people, this is a red flag. Many of you have the greatest counsel at your fingertips—your parents! For those in college, your greatest advocate is a phone call away. If you are out in the job force, a lunch with Mom or Dad could be life-changing. Still living at home with the folks? You have it made since the access is so easy. Others might not have the privilege of a godly mom or dad to bounce things off of. What about a mentor, pastor, teacher? Someone will walk with you through this. You don't know what hangs in the balance if you don't.

If you are not seeking this advice, is it because you already know the answer and do not want to hear it? You might avoid these conversations with a parent or mentor because it requires work or effort on your part. Whatever the reason, if you are not pursuing deep conversations with God, parents, or mentors, your journey might be headed into rough waters, waters of regret.

A Good Answer

The final answer to Question #2—*Why do I want to be in a relationship with him or her?*—is a longer one. When asked, "Why him or her?" you should be able to respond with, "Let me count the ways!" and proceed to rattle off a list of who that person is and why it is you like her or him. If you cannot do this, it is obvious you are lying to yourself and need to reevaluate your motives for dating.

What do you think so far? How are you doing? Are you being honest with yourself? Maybe you just need to put the bookmark in, and get to know the person you want to date a little better before you move on. Maybe you need to listen to that tug on your heart and forget about ever dating this person. Maybe it is a relationship you have

The Second Question: Prove It

been in for years and you need to call it off...today. Or maybe you need to praise God for granting you such an incredible person to be in a relationship with.

Listen to that tug on your heart, but do me a favor and make sure you are ready to take that plunge. Do not break up through a text in the next five minutes, and then crawl back into the relationship tomorrow. Do not short change yourself. You deserve to take your time and fully think through the next step in this.

Getting Personal

One night, I was praying about my situation with Brittany. I wrote out my prayer in a journal, talking to God about all the things I had learned about this girl. The list piled up quickly of who this girl was, and before I knew it, I realized I was not lying to myself about her. She was amazing, and I was surprised at how well I had gotten to know her through mutual friends, serving alongside her in ministry, and our group hangouts.

I wrote things like "gifted in encouragement," "kind-hearted," "patient," "fun-loving," "loves people," "ministry-minded," "thoughtful," "selfless," and much, much more. I constantly saw how encouraging she was, and I loved seeing her use her gifts to bless others. I also valued a girl who could hold her own in a crowd. She had to be a people person or else she would hate dating me. To be honest, I am not near as much of a people person as she is. People *want* to be around her. She is the life of the party. She was so patient and loving, and this was clearly a fruit of the Spirit evident in her. I knew that to date me she would have to have a doctorate in patience.

The tough part was that I had been infatuated with girls before, but I had no idea what it meant to be in love. I might not have known it at the time, but I was sifting through years of emotions, failures, and well-intentioned setbacks. I was thinking through why I liked her because I did not trust myself. To this day I have kept that page marked in my prayer journal. That day was the day I truly fell in love with a girl who was more than I had ever dreamed up. I just did not know it yet.

As if telling God were not enough, I drove around town with my best friend, Brandon, the next day, and I could not help telling him all the wonderful things about Brittany. I updated him in much detail about everything I had prayed through the day before and how I had finally come to a point of genuinely liking this girl for who she was. After much conversation Brandon quickly asked, "Why do you not ask her out?"

I felt like I was being stopped in my tracks. Doubt entered my mind, and I shrank back into fear of the unknown. Honestly, it was the fear of not knowing what a relationship with her would look like. I backpedaled a little in the conversation and expressed to him a few things I was unsure about. I felt I needed more time. It was clear that with time, I fell more "in like" with her, but there was still a sort of reservation I could not put my finger on. Maybe I could not see it, but my best buddy could. Because Brandon was frustrated with our conversation, he asked me what is now my third question. It was during that car ride that the third question was developed.

Reflection Questions on *Why do you want to be in a relationship with him or her?*

Do you see any of these or other potential red flags with this person? If so, list them here:

The Second Question: Prove It

List the top three things about this person that inspire you to want to date him or her:

_____

_____

_____

Do you need to change the current "window" you are in? If so, which one and how?

_____

_____

_____

How are you "in like" with this person and not infatuated?

_____

_____

_____

THE THIRD QUESTION: THE DOOZY

Getting Personal

As I drove around town that day with Brandon, I was on a roll, chatting about how awesome this girl was and telling Brandon about my journey through these first two questions (which I had not even fully developed yet). I was raving about her, exploring my doubts, and smiling ear to ear. Brandon was being a good friend, just listening.

The thing I always appreciate about my friendship with Brandon is that we communicate openly and honestly. Back in our business days, our attorney advised against making a fifty-fifty partnership, saying it would never work. He told us someone needed to be in charge and have the power. We went against that advice and thrived. We thrived because of the honest communication we shared. However, in this certain moment, as I poured out my thoughts about Brittany, Brandon's honesty stung a bit.

I was in the middle of explaining my journey when Brandon interrupted me, "Hey, I've got a question for you," he said.

"Anything—fire away," I replied.

The Third Question: The Doozy

"Well, you have told me all of this stuff about her, but my question is, who the heck are you?"

I had no reply. I stayed silent, slightly frustrated. I was taken aback and slightly appalled at his question. Even though I was sort of hurt, I realized this was the final piece for me. I realized in that moment that I was not afraid to ask Brittany out because I thought she would say "no." I was not afraid to ask her out because I feared she would not be who I thought she was. I was afraid because I thought she would say "yes," and then I would not be the person *she* thought *I* was.

The Third Question

The last question I want you to ask yourself is this:

Why would the person want to date me?

This is by far the most important question of the three. I want you to not only be able to answer this question but answer it confidently. The set of questions below gets you headed down the right path.

I must tell you I purposely worded the questions to be a bit unfair. I realize you cannot put your relationship with God on a scale, but for our purposes, knowing that God loves you unconditionally, just be honest with yourself. It is time to shift the focus from the other person, to you. Write down your thoughts in the space provided:

On a scale from 1 to 10, how honorable would most people say you are?

1 2 3 4 5 6 7 8 9 10

On a scale from 1 to 10, how trustworthy would most people say you are?

1 2 3 4 5 6 7 8 9 10

On a scale from 1 to 10, how would your parents rate you on your "date-ability?"

1 2 3 4 5 6 7 8 9 10

On a scale from 1 to 10, how well do you treat people?

1 2 3 4 5 6 7 8 9 10

On a scale from 1 to 10, how do you rate your last relationship?

1 2 3 4 5 6 7 8 9 10

On a scale from 1 to 10, how would your past significant other rate your last relationship?

1 2 3 4 5 6 7 8 9 10

On a scale from 1 to 10, how are you doing at honoring Christ in your personal life?

1 2 3 4 5 6 7 8 9 10

If I asked your best friend your top three qualities, what would he or she say?

1. _____

2. _____

3. _____

The Third Question: The Doozy

In dating relationships today, so much attention is placed on "interviewing" others as our dating candidates. Well-intentioned or not, it naturally takes the focus off our own hearts. Even if you can walk through the first two questions with perfect motives, you still have not looked at the most important part—yourself.

Though this is the last question, you have work to do. This is the most important question you'll answer in this entire book.

In the space below, list some reasons you could give to this person's parents if they asked you, "Why should we let you date our son or daughter?"

1. _____

2. _____

3. _____

4. _____

5. _____

6. _____

7. _____

8. _____

9. _____

10. _____

It feels a little arrogant to do that, doesn't it? I'll bet some of you did not even write anything—you just read ahead to see what I would say! Just be honest. Go back and try again if you need to, but be honest. Think in these terms if you are having trouble—picture a trusted friend or mentor coming to you and asking this question. What would you tell him or her? Go back and write down a list of reasons someone should date you.

Early on in my walk with Christ, my friend Joe shared with me a little exercise I often adapted in my prayer journal as I talked with the Lord. I want to share this with you now in hopes it might shed some light on your own physical, emotional, and spiritual health. Think about your life in those three areas: 1) physical, 2) emotional, and 3) spiritual. Think of each area as a cup. Each day you are constantly filled or emptied in each of these areas. Over time, your cups get depleted or overflow. Using the images below, color in each cup according to where you are in each of these areas. Try not to be deceived by a certain mood. Step back, and be objective.

HOW FULL DO YOU FEEL?

SPIRITUAL   EMOTIONAL   PHYSICAL

The Third Question: The Doozy

Now let's put these three exercises together. Look back at the questions you answered using the 1-through-10 scale and the reasons you would give parents as to why their child should date you. Look back at both lists and see if they match up. Do they actually support each other? Does how you rated your own view of yourself equate to what you think parents want to hear? Now add in the cup exercise. Specifically, look at the Spiritual one. Is it full? Does the level of the cup match with the first two exercises?

In the space below, write out the top three things you "fear" about yourself or that you feel are "lacking" in yourself. Maybe these are the things you listed earlier that do not seem to match up. Maybe they reflect an insecurity you have. Perhaps they are simply issues you have uncovered about yourself while reading this book.

1. _____

2. _____

3. _____

Discover a good answer to Question #3 by reading Colossians 3:1–4:

> *If then you have been raised with Christ, seek the things that are above, where Christ is, seated at the right hand of God. Set your minds on things that are above, not on things that are on earth. For you have died, and your life is hidden with Christ in God. When Christ who is your life appears, then you also will appear with him in glory.*

What does it mean that we are "raised with Christ," as noted above?

_____

_____

If we are not seeking the things above, then what are we seeking? Think about the big, round ball on which you live...

_____

_____

If I seek these things instead of heavenly things, what might I look for to fulfill me?

_____

_____

Why should we seek things that are in Colossians 3:1-4?

_____

_____

What should your life be hidden in? To gain more insight, read through these verses that help us understand Colossians 3, and then write in the space that follows the scriptures:

Isaiah 49:2
He made my mouth like a sharp sword;

The Third Question: The Doozy

   in the shadow of his hand he hid me;
he made me a polished arrow;
   in his quiver he hid me away.

Psalm 27:5–6
For he will hide me in his shelter
   in the day of trouble;
he will conceal me under the cover of his tent;
   he will lift me high upon a rock.
And now my head shall be lifted up
   above my enemies all around me,
and I will offer in his tent
   sacrifices with shouts of joy;
I will sing and make melody to the Lord.

Psalm 31:19–20
Oh, how abundant is your goodness,
   which you have stored up for those who fear you
and worked for those who take refuge in you,
   in the sight of the children of mankind!
In the cover of your presence you hide them
   from the plots of men;
you store them in your shelter
   from the strife of tongues.

_____

_____

Who is "my life" in Colossians 3:4?

_____

_____

Why is this important?

_____

_____

If Christ is not your life, then what can take His place?

_____

_____

I hope you just got hammered by this like I did. Your answer to Question #3 is that *Christ is your life!* Your mind is set on heavenly things. How else do you expect to be a "good" boyfriend or girlfriend to a person? Who cares about the boundaries you set up if you have no reason to set them up?

Consider another angle. My wife and I have Philippians 2:4–5 inscribed on our wedding rings, and I often revisit these verses. I revisit them often because I often drift back into a self-centered view of my relationship with her:

> *Do nothing from rivalry or conceit, but in humility count others more significant than yourselves. Let each of you look not only to his own interests, but also to the interests of others. Have this mind among yourselves, which is yours in Christ Jesus.*

What does it mean to "count others more significant than yourselves"?

_____

_____

The Third Question: The Doozy

What is "this mind" the scripture references?

_____

_____

How do you get "this mind"?

_____

_____

The mind or attitude Paul is talking about in this scripture is a mind of selfless commitment. It is a mind that truly allows us to love. This is the mind and attitude I constantly want to have toward my wife. While I wish I could, I cannot have this mind in and of myself alone. I can manipulate it, fake it awhile, and talk about it, but I cannot truly have it without Christ.

This is a reflection, an outworking of what it means to be hidden in Christ—I consider my wife more important than myself. You also must have "this mind," because you get it from having a relationship with Christ.

Now, let me tell you the best part of the verse. If you have a Bible, you either have a different translation of verse 5 or a little note saying it can read another way. The other way it can be read from the original language is this:

Having this mind among yourselves, which was also in Christ Jesus.

This was the mind and attitude of the Savior! This is Jesus' example of humble service. He is the one who considered your interests greater than His own, and He willingly laid His life down for you. This is the gospel. My sin put on Him, and in exchange, I receive the righteousness of the Father. The wrath of God is no longer meant for me, but put on the Son. This is what it looks like to live "hidden" in Him. This is how I can truly love. This is how I can consider others more significant than myself—I know what it is to be forgiven, loved, and captured by a sacrificial deity.

Paul continues as he shows us the example of Christ in Philippians 2:6–9:

> *Who, though he was in the form of God, did not count equality with God a thing to be grasped, but emptied himself, by taking the form of a servant, being born in the likeness of men. And being found in human form, he humbled himself by becoming obedient to the point of death, even death on a cross. Therefore God has highly exalted him and bestowed on him the name that is above every name.*

Was or is Jesus God?

_____

_____

What "form" did He take on?

_____

_____

What was Jesus's "act of obedience" that is referenced?

_____

_____

The Third Question: The Doozy

How did Jesus set an example of humility and looking to the interests of others?

_____

_____

To whom was Jesus being obedient?

_____

_____

If Jesus was being obedient to the Father, was he dying to glorify man or God?

_____

_____

Sometimes this text is referred to as the "kenosis" of Christ, which means Jesus emptied Himself. He left His royal dwellings in heaven and took on the form of a lowly servant on earth. He did this so He might take on sin and redeem mankind at the cross.

Bruce Shelley says in his book *Church History in Plain Language*, "Christianity is the only major religion to have as its central event the humiliation of its God."

If you know the story of Jesus in the Garden of Gethsemane, you see Jesus' others-oriented mind here as well. Jesus prays in the garden in the final hours before he is arrested and led to slaughter. He prays, and the Bible tells us he is in great distress. He makes this statement that forever rings in my ears. Check this out in Matthew 26:38–39:

> *Then he said to them, "My soul is very sorrowful, even to death; remain here, and watch with me." And going a little farther he fell on his face and prayed, saying, "My Father, if it be possible, let this cup pass from me; nevertheless, not as I will, but as you will."*

We clearly see the pain He is going through, and I wonder what was going on in the mind of Jesus, who is both fully God and fully man. Was He picturing me, and did my life flash through His mind? Did He see me suffering the wrath of God if He were not to go to the cross? What pain was He experiencing?

One important thing to understand is that Jesus did not fear death. He had power over death, and he knew it, so this was not the fear. The fear was found in this "cup." This cup was the full wrath of God poured out onto sin. This cup was meant for you and me, this wrath of God was rightly meant for us! This cup, this wrath, is what Jesus took and absorbed into himself. This act of Jesus taking this cup was a Philippians 2 mind or attitude. At some level, Jesus humbled himself to a point of death and in that act he considered me more significant by taking the wrath of God for me.

It is not that you and I are more significant than Jesus. Rather, Jesus was being obedient to the Father to restore the creation to a place of worship. Jesus was out to glorify God alone. Experiencing the wrath of His Father was something Jesus had never done before, but He was willing to do it so others might be restored to the position of living lives that glorify God. Jesus sought God's glory above all, but He did it by emptying himself and dying for his enemies.

If you never understand this gospel, this good news of what Jesus did, then how are you ever going to love someone to the fullest? If you never feel or experience love like this, how will you ever know what love truly feels like? I urge you to consider your ways, and consider Christ.

Going Deeper

Let's explore some potential red flags to consider if *you* are in a good position to date.

Red Flag: You think he or she will make you a better person

While this might seem like a flattering reason to date, if you want to date someone because they will "make you a better person," I suggest you evaluate this. You could be looking for them to be your savior, while your true Savior does not need another to make you a "better person." A "better person" is one who is sanctified, meaning you look less like you and more like Jesus. If you are going to quit cussing or smoking for someone else and therefore be "a better person," you probably are not in a position to date.

Do not misunderstand me and think I am saying the person you are dating should not encourage and inspire you to be better. I am saying you are only made "better" through Christ. Paul speaks to this in 1 Corinthians 7:32–35, about focus and an undivided devotion to the Lord. Read this passage below and make some observations:

> *I want you to be free from anxieties. The unmarried man is anxious about the things of the Lord, how to please the Lord. But the married man is anxious about worldly things, how to please his wife, and his interests are divided. And the unmarried or betrothed woman is anxious about the things of the Lord, how to be holy in body and spirit. But*

Dating Is Not for Marriage

the married woman is anxious about worldly things, how to please her husband. I say this for your own benefit, not to lay any restraint upon you, but to promote good order and to secure your undivided devotion to the Lord.

In 1 Corinthians 7:32-35, what types of anxieties might Paul be referring to in the first sentence?

_____

_____

What about the anxieties in the second sentence?

_____

_____

Compare and contrast the married to the unmarried person as described above:

_____

_____

When you read the verses above, understand it is in the context of marriage and follows Paul telling the Corinthians he wishes they all had the gift of celibacy (no desire to be married or sexually active) like he had as shared in 1 Corinthians 7:6-7. However, I believe this same concept can apply to a dating relationship.

If you cannot answer this third question well and continue in your pursuit of that relationship, consider this warning from Paul. Paul's point is simple—if you have a

The Third Question: The Doozy

husband or wife, your interest is divided. If you do not, you simply have to focus only on the things of the Lord.

If you are in a place where you cannot confidently boast in God's grace in your life and how you are hidden in Christ with God, then a relationship with another person is not where you need to invest your energy. This is not to say both your relationship with the Lord and your relationship with another person cannot grow at the same time, but think about the emotional energy you are going to put forth for that guy or girl.

To focus energy on a dating relationship is definitely not a bad thing, but what if instead of focusing that energy on your relationship with a person you were to focus it on a relationship with the eternal God? What if your prayer journal was filled with things God is growing in you? What if conversations with your parents or a mentor were about how God sanctifies you and what He reveals about Himself to you? What if you were to stay awake at night praying for the things of God in your life and your thoughts were consumed with that?

What about your physical energy? If you have a boyfriend or a girlfriend, you are going to spend more time with that person. At least once a week, you will probably end up on a date with that person, and daily you will find yourself communicating somehow. You will show up to games, have dinner with the other's family, and hopefully even attend church together. Again, these are all great things, but what if things with you and the Lord are on the rocks and you are spending all your physical energy with that other person? What if you have an opportunity to serve at your church but do not do it because of all the time you spend with that other person? What if you had an opportunity to go on a mission trip but because that other person could not go, you chose not to go either? If you were single, you would serve, you would go, and you would be able to spend much more of your physical energy on growing in the Lord.

If you can answer Question #3 well, you can surely do both, but only after you can honestly answer it—which I will plainly describe later. Most people who do this well are people who spend their physical, emotional, and mental energy on the things of God as if they were not dating at all. This is the person who signs up for the mission trip without even knowing if a boyfriend or girlfriend is going. This is the person who shows up to church even if the other person does not. This is the person who serves at church at the expense of the couple's "church experience" together. This is not rude but rather an action that proves their love of God.

So maybe you are reading this and you just do not want to date right now? Paul would say, "Fantastic!" You can serve the Lord with fewer distractions that way!

Red Flag: You think you can make them happy, and that they will make you happy

This is a lot of pressure. If you think you are able to make the other person happy, you are right, but not completely. The part you do not see right now is that your ability to make them happy quickly wears off, and when it does, the person will break up with you because you have failed him or her. We are all human. Therefore, we all fail one another sooner or later.

If your main concern is making the other person happy, this reflects a heart that is rooted in pleasing people over pleasing God. If you are bent on pleasing someone else, you will fail, and they will not be pleased. If you are focused on pleasing God, you can succeed through grace and, in turn, allow God to be fully satisfying to the other person. We must all realize God alone can fill this void in us. As the famous saying from John Piper goes, "God is most glorified in us, when we are most satisfied in Him." God alone can satisfy.

Read this passage from Jeremiah 17:5–8:

> *Thus says the Lord: "Cursed is the man who trusts in man and makes flesh his strength, whose heart turns away from the Lord. He is like a shrub in the desert, and shall not see any good come. He shall dwell in the parched places of the wilderness, in an uninhabited salt land. Blessed is the man who trusts in the Lord, whose trust is the Lord. He is like a tree planted by water, that sends out its roots by the stream, and does not fear when heat comes, for its leaves remain green, and is not anxious in the year of drought, for it does not cease to bear fruit."*

This is a great verse to meditate on when it comes to those of us who are prone to people-pleasing. Notice how the first man finds his strength in flesh and is more concerned about what's worldly than the godly. This is someone who is "trusting" in a relationship to make him happy.

If you are trusting in a relationship for joy, peace, comfort, identity, or anything along those lines, you are a people-pleaser. You will do whatever it takes to "please" that person so he or she will give you the desired outcome you seek. Take a minute to understand how Jeremiah describes this person.

List the two ways the person in verse 5 is described in the above piece of scripture:

_____

_____

In what or whom does this person trust?

_____

_____

Why do you think he is "cursed"?

_____

_____

What is the outcome of his hope in verse 6?

_____

_____

Why do you think there is no "life" found in verse 6?

_____

_____

_____

Would you say you sometimes feel like this shrub in a relationship?

_____

_____

_____

The Third Question: The Doozy

List the one way the person in verse 7 is described:

_____

_____

In what or whom does this person trust?

_____

_____

What are the two things this person is not, as noted in verse 8?

_____

_____

Do you find yourself constantly anxious about a relationship?

_____

_____

    This passage reveals so much about whom you are seeking to please. If you answered "yes" to that last question, consider if you are in the place of the first person in verses 5–6. Maybe your trust is in that person you are dating or wanting to date, and not in God. Notice also the specific wording is not, "trust *in* the Lord," but rather it reads, "trust *is* the Lord." This means He alone is trustworthy. We do not just trust in what He can do or what He can give us—we trust in who He is.

Red Flag: You ignore wise counsel

Who in your life could you bring into a situation to look at it from an outsider's perspective? Proverbs 15:22 says, "Plans fail for lack of counsel, but with many advisers they succeed." If only there were some people in your life who were older than you, experienced in relationships, loved you more than anyone else on earth, and had your best interests in mind.

It would be nice if those people cared so much for you that they had actually changed your diapers. Oh, wait, you do have those people! I do not care how old you are, your parents or loving guardians who raised you are a great resource. Unfortunately I know this actually is not true for all of us. But find someone you can bring into your situation to help you sift through the rubble and make the best decision possible.

If you are unwilling to bring in this wise counsel, then just go ahead and admit you already know what you should do but are not willing to do it.

A Good Answer

A good answer to Question #3—*Why would the person want to date me?*—is this: "I am hidden in Christ."

Ultimately you need to be able to say, "I know I am hidden in Christ as in Colossians 1 and 3, and I hope to glorify God *in* and *through* this relationship." This is the answer you must find peace with in your heart. Most of us fail to see the problem with broken relationships or misguided intentions is really about ourselves.

You and I are sinners. We are incapable of achieving a God-centered relationship on our own. We must rely on the Spirit of God and be hidden in Christ. This is why you must be hidden in Christ, as your hope, motivation, and compass. If you are not hidden in Christ, why would you pursue a relationship with a guy or girl?

To be hidden in Christ simply means that when people see you, they see Christ beaming from you. You are like the moon, reflecting the light of the sun. You reflect Christ. Your obedience to Christ is evident, your life is one that produces fruit and displays Christ to others. When people look at you, can they see a reflection of Christ?

Getting Personal

After Brandon urged me to ask myself that third question—*Why would the person want to date me?*—I went home and spent some time reading and praying. I felt really set back by Brandon's question, and I was not sure how to answer it. I had spent all this time worrying so much about Brittany that I had almost forgotten the most important part. My own heart, as related to God, was in question.

That night, I happened to be reading Psalm 51. This Psalm is David's response about a year after his sin with Bathsheba and Uriah. David had slept with Uriah's wife, Bathsheba, and then murdered Uriah to cover it up. Psalm 51:12 says:

Restore to me the joy of your salvation, and uphold me with a willing spirit.

As I was reading this passage, I took out my pen I always use to take notes in my Bible. That day I made a note beside this verse, and I will never forget it. Even as I write this sentence, I am reading this passage from that Bible and to the left of the column it reads, "V.12—Restore my first love to me." I continued my thought out to the right side of the same verse and I wrote to God, "I have no business pursuing other relationships when ours lies in ruin."

> 12 and take not ⁹your Holy Spirit from me.
> Restore to me the joy of your salvation,
> and uphold me with a willing spirit.
> 13 Then I will teach transgressors your ways,
> and sinners will ʳreturn to you.
> 14 Deliver me from ʰbloodguiltiness, O God,
> O ʲGod of my salvation,

Handwritten margin notes: I have no business ministering to others of their relationship with God while mine lies in ruin. 5/13/08 — I have no business pursuing other relationships when ours lies in ruin. 5.13.08

From that moment on, all bets were off. It was about me pursuing the Lord and not worrying so much about pursuing Brittany. I prayed that God would have her date someone else as I focused my thoughts on Him. This was honestly one of the hardest prayers I've ever prayed, but I knew my heart was in no place to date. I really did not want her to date someone else, but I knew I desperately needed the Lord to finish shaping my heart in this area.

On June 13, 2008, after a long week of being involved in a sports camp that hosted almost a thousand kids, I offered to drive Brittany to her car. She was one of our hired staff that week, and as I parked next to her car, I started a conversation. "Brittany, can I ask two things of you?" I asked, a bit reserved.

"Sure," she said, wracking her brain about what it could be.

"First, I need to ask your forgiveness. Over the past few months, I feel like I have crossed a few small boundaries and led you on a little bit. Please forgive me if I have done that in any way."

She did not really answer much past a "sure, no problem." She sat in silence, awaiting the next question. I did not hesitate.

"Second, I want to know what you are doing next weekend because I would love to take you on a date. I have an idea I think would be really fun."

Brittany said "yes" to me that day, and the rest is history. I took her to the flagship Starbucks in Dallas in honor of our weekly "accidental" meetings at Starbucks in Denton. We sat and shared more about who we were and had a great time together. I was finally confident that I was not out for my own selfish gain, as I was motivated to date her because of who she was. I could list a thousand things about why I liked her and not some other girl, and I could honestly say I was hidden in Christ. It was clear this was different. It was not different because of any other factor—it was different because I was where I needed to be, in my heart, with the Lord.

Reflection Questions on *Why would the person want to date me?*

In your own words, describe what it means to be "hidden in Christ":

_____

_____

What would you say is one area of your life that doesn't reflect Christ?

_____

_____

Name one person from whom you could seek wise counsel:

_____

_____

What would you write out beside Psalm 51:12?

_____

SECTION 3

A NEW LENS

THE RELATIONSHIP LENS

Y ou are most likely in one of two spots. You are dating someone and are reading this book in an effort to date more consciously, or you are considering dating someone and want some help jumping in. Either way, chances are you want to date well. Like I said in the beginning, this book is not a formula. It is meant to inspire you to search your heart. The relationship you are currently pursuing is not something you should take lightly. What if you, through God's grace, are able to have a successful relationship before it starts or even a successful one if you have to break it off? Success depends on the lens you view it through.

One day I was talking with John, a great friend and gifted counselor, about dating relationships. We talked specifically about teenage dating. I was really encouraged by a statement he made. As we talked about how to best shepherd young people through the dating process, John said something I thought was very clever and simple. He said, "You know what no spouse ever says to the other? No spouse ever looks at the other and says, 'Wow, I am so glad you dated all those people before me. I am so glad you had so many girlfriends or boyfriends in high school. Those have made you such a better spouse to me. Thank you for dating everybody possible before you met me.'"

I laughed as he said it because it is so true. The gravity of the relationship you are currently pursuing is huge. There are so many ways to fail when dating by the world's standards and very few ways to succeed. However, the world doesn't judge success and failure for us, God does. I urge you to redefine your goal of dating to honoring Christ both *in* and *through* that relationship. Then honestly ask yourself these three questions:

1. Why do I want to date?

2. Why do I want to date him or her?

3. Why would the person want to date me?

If you have a selfish motivation for dating and pursue a relationship, it is a time bomb waiting for the perfect moment to explode. Selfishly motivated relationships never work, because God created successful relationships to be about Him, not about you!

Think about it this way. The average person in the United States lives to be about seventy-eight years old. This means you will spend about 28,470 days on earth. Of those 28,470 days you will be alive, you will spend about the first 4,380 days not really thinking about relationships with the opposite sex. That leaves you 24,090 days when you will potentially be interested in a relationship. Of those 24,090 days, there will be about 3,650 to account for your middle school, high school, and college days. What you might fail to see is that there are a remaining 20,440 days you will most likely spend with your spouse. So many people are willing to forgo those 20,440 days for the 3,650 days. We tend to act on our emotions and end up dating for poor reasons that lead to scars we will carry with us into those 20,440 days.

The Relationship Lens

The decision you are currently working through will affect 20,440 days of your life. Maybe the decision you are working through is related to that person with whom you will spend 20,440 days.

This decision shapes your choice of a future spouse. It shapes what your premarital counseling looks like, what your honeymoon night looks like, and maybe even the way you communicate with each other. It shapes the stories you'll tell your kids someday and the advice you'll give them. It impacts your relationships with your siblings and parents, for better or for worse. It changes the friendships around you.

Let me say this as plainly as I know how: there is a certain "lens" you must put on for any of this to make sense. Without this lens none of the questions matter and none of them are helpful. I hope this book has stirred in you a lens through which to view all things. The lens through which you see something is key to determining if you should be in that relationship or not. This lens guides any decision you make, and you will constantly be tempted to drift from this lens. I battle viewing life through this very same lens—the lens of the gospel.

Paul says this in 2 Corinthians 5:18–21:

> *All this is from God, who through Christ reconciled us to himself and gave us the ministry of reconciliation; that is, in Christ God was reconciling the world to himself, not counting their trespasses against them, and entrusting to us the message of reconciliation. Therefore, we are ambassadors for Christ, God making his appeal through us. We implore you on behalf of Christ, be reconciled to God. For our sake he made him to*

> be sin who knew no sin, so that in him we
> might become the righteousness of God.

The gospel itself is a story of a reconciled relationship. It is the broken relationship I had with God because of my sin and the good news of His mending this broken relationship through the sacrifice of His Son. Still this sin knocks at my door, and I'm tempted to live with a Jason-centered lens. Daily I battle this urge to be out for my glory, my fame. I battle viewing life through the lens of "me." Daily the battle between God being the center of my world versus me being the center of my world constantly rages in my mind. Daily I am challenged to live simply by the gospel alone. This gospel is what allows us to live in a relationship with someone in the first place. How would you survive in relationship without forgiveness? God created forgiveness, and in fact, He was the first to act in forgiveness.

The gospel, plainly put, is the good news of Jesus Christ, that He would come and invade human history to save people who were unable to save themselves. You and I were created for God's glory, as His image bearers. Then the first sin came. The fall of Adam and Eve is what we call "original sin." Through one man, Adam, sin entered the world, and all of us, descendants of Adam, inherit that sin. Sin means we have missed the mark of God's holiness and fall short of His standards.

We are born in sin. We are born with the natural desire to look out for ourselves, to seek gain on our own behalf. We are naturally inclined to judge for ourselves what is best. This is the very thing Adam and Eve fell into in the Garden of Eden. They desired to judge for themselves what was right and what was wrong. No longer would they have to trust in God's law and His words. Adam and Eve fell, and in that, so did we. We fell in the sense that no longer would we naturally live for God's glory but for our own. That moment resulted in no longer being able to trust ourselves for salvation. It would take a divine act from the outside to fix what we had done.

God had a plan for redemption all along. There was no "Plan B." In Genesis 3:15, God talks to the serpent, Satan, and says this:

> *I will put enmity between you and the woman, and between your offspring and her offspring; he shall bruise your head, and you shall bruise his heel.*

Immediately upon the fall of mankind, God intends to restore the creation that has sinned against Him. He tells Satan a singular offspring will come from a woman and that there will be hostility between the two. This offspring will be both fully God and fully man, invading the very essence of mankind. God's plan is for Him to come and deal a defeating blow to Satan's head. He is going to conquer sin and death through Jesus.

God is saying to Satan, "You will strike his heal and wound him temporarily, but he will strike your head and permanently defeat you." This is what is known as the "protoevangelion" or the "first gospel." This is the first time the good news of Jesus is mentioned in the Bible—Jesus would come to earth, and Satan would hand Him over to the torture chamber of a cross for crucifixion. Yet Jesus will rise from the grave three days later to conquer death and Satan in one fell swoop. Sin will no longer have power over mankind, and freedom will be offered.

The righteousness of God demands justice. As an all-knowing, all-loving, perfect God, He cannot allow sin to remain unpunished. This is why Jesus had to go to the cross in the first place. This is why in the Garden of Gethsemane, He knows He will drink the cup of God's wrath. This is why He suffers as a human. This is why He is thirsty, why He cries, why He is tempted. In every way He experiences our lives, yet lives a perfect life.

In the finality of his sacrifice, He places His perfect life up on a cross in exchange for our nasty one. In an instant, we are forever changed for believing in this gospel. Beyond this is no good news at all. This is the lens through which you must view every aspect of your life. This is the lens of grace, forgiveness, wrath satisfied, free from sin. Specifically, this is the lens through which you must view your current or future relationship. Without the lens of the gospel, it is impossible to have a correct view.

If I were to ask you to write down your top five priorities, what would they be? Go ahead and write them out in the space below.

1. _____

2. _____

3. _____

4. _____

5. _____

I'll bet if you are a follower of Jesus, you put either "God" or "Jesus" as your number-one priority. Most likely "family" came in at number two, like any good son or daughter might write. Then, some of you probably put "friends" or "school" at numbers three and four, and then rounded it off with your job, a sport, an instrument, or some other activity. Those are not bad priorities, but I suggest a minor shift. What if I said Jesus should *not* be your number-one priority?

Let me clarify. If Jesus is your number-one priority, you have a tendency to place him in a to-do list. Because you put Jesus at number one, you go to church, read your Bible, and pray often. Check! You are done with your first priority, and you can move on to the second. By the time you get to your second priority, you have forgotten that Jesus should not simply be a priority, but rather *the lens through which you view all priorities.*

If Jesus is a lens instead of a priority, when you spend time with your family, you do so in a loving, selfless, forgiving, kind, generous way. You are able to do this because of the way you view things, through the lens of Jesus and the gospel. When you play your sport, you take this same lens with you and apply it to that sport. It now drives how you treat your teammates and coaches, and motivates you to work hard.

One day I borrowed a friends' fancy camera, and it took all of my brain power to figure out how to turn it on. Although it had fancy settings and lenses, I had no idea which lens was on the camera, but I was in charge of taking pictures at the event. All night, I worked that camera, gathering people together, shooting awesome action shots, and capturing cool moments. The following week, when we looked through the pictures, everybody was getting mad at me. "What did I do wrong?" I asked defensively.

"You forgot to change the lens, and all the pictures are terrible!" they said.

I did not realize I was taking all those pictures through the wrong lens. I still do not know what I did wrong!

This is what becomes of us sometimes when it comes to relationships. We are looking through the lens of "me," when we should be looking through the lens of the gospel. This is my hope for you as you make your way through the Three Question Gauntlet, that you now view that relationship through the lens of Christ instead of the lens of "me." If it were up to either you or God to make the best out of that relationship, who would you bet on? If it were up to either you or God to determine if you should be dating that person or not, who would you listen to?

Faith vs. Fear

The choice is yours. Give the real reason, and write it below when you ask yourself, *Why do I want to be in a dating relationship?* Give one answer.

_____

_____

How do you like your answer? Does it fit within the lens of the gospel?

If you put "because of him or her," then, *why do you want to date that person?* Write your reasons in five words.

1. _____

2. _____

3. _____

4. _____

5. _____

Are you trying to sell yourself on the idea of being in a relationship, or are you being genuine? If you can honestly put down five Christ-honoring words, then do one last thing and explain *why that person should want to date you?* Give it in one sentence.

The Relationship Lens

I have one more thing for you to do. Take the things you wrote above, and talk to a parent, mentor, or youth pastor, showing them what you wrote. Ask them to call it like they see it and give you some advice on what to do.

At this point, you will act in one of two ways—faith or fear. Fear is a lack of faith. Fear is how you will act if you feel you cannot live without that person or you feel scared the person will date someone else. Fear is what you feel if you are scared to date because you are going to "mess up." Fear could mean you are so concerned about pleasing people that you have forgotten about pleasing God.

Faith means you trust God. Faith could be you calling him or her right now and ending a relationship you are in that is centered around sin. Faith could be you trusting God to help you stop obsessing over him or her. Faith means you pursue a relationship with the Creator, rather than the quarterback of the football team or the captain of the cheer team. I do not know where you fall, but I do know you have a choice. Act in faith.

My favorite professor of all time at Dallas Seminary was Dr. James Allman. I took him for every class I could, and I will never forget how he defined faith for us. He explained to us that faith starts as *knowledge*. This knowledge is in the person and the plan of God. This knowledge is rooted in the Bible and discovered throughout one's life experiences. Knowledge, however, is not faith.

Somewhere along the way, we experience the *assent* of knowledge. This is when we truly believe what we already know. This is Thomas looking at the wounds of Jesus after his resurrection and proclaiming, "My Lord and my God!" Dr. Allman points out that these first two steps are merely educational or cognitive, while the following two are affective, meaning they involve feelings or attitudes. A cognitive response just deals with the mind—it is a beginning, but as Jesus teaches during the Sermon on the Mount in Matthew chapters 5–7, it must get to a heart level. This heart level is the affective—feeling or attitude.

Dr. Allman continued his diagram on the white board. He wrote the words *love relationship*. Then he wrote out 1 Peter 1:8, which reads, "Though you have not seen him, you love him. Though you do not now see him, you believe in him and rejoice with joy that is inexpressible and filled with glory."

Our professor continued to point out to us the parallelism between loving and believing. Because of this love relationship, there is a change in behavior.

All love relationships lead to a change in our behavior, whether for good or bad. This is true of family relationships and even the one that caused you to buy this book. In a healthy relationship, these changes are always for the better. Specifically with Jesus, it is *because* of this love relationship that we change. Immediately upon salvation, God begins a process of what is called sanctification—making us look more like Jesus and less like ourselves.

Sanctification is a process of change. First, your heart is changed, and you are now in a love relationship with Jesus. Therefore, you desire obedience and a change in your behavior. Second, a love relationship leads to taking risks. You put yourself at risk for the ones you love. This is why a mother instinctively lays down her life for her child, or a husband puts himself in harm's way so his wife is safe. This is why, in a dating relationship, you are willing to go out on a limb and take risks that involve the other person.

With God we take risks. We give up things, people, places, money, fame, or whatever He calls us away from. As we take risks, we immediately experience the next aspect

The Relationship Lens

of faith, which is *hope*. We have hope that the person we are in a love relationship with will be there for us in times of need.

Faith is gaining *knowledge* of the person and plan of God, and nurturing that knowledge into an *assent* that causes us to truly believe in what we already know. From there, we enter into a *love relationship* with God because of our belief in who He is. This love relationship leads us to a changed behavior and allows us to take risks based on our knowledge and the assent of that knowledge. Upon taking those risks, we *hope* in the person and the plan of God, and then our faith grows.

By taking healthy risks, we learn how trustworthy God truly is, and trust more in the person and plan of God. This affects our love relationship with God, and we learn to love Him more. By loving Him more, we take more risks, knowing He provides. This only further proves God's promises and faithfulness, giving us all the more hope in who He is. This is faith! Thanks, Dr. Allman.

So what about you? Are you acting in faith or fear? Through what lens do you currently view your relationship? Have you successfully navigated the Three Question Gauntlet? Have you made your decision? Take the risk. See what God does.

The truth is that you know in your heart what you should do, and now you just have to do it. Even if your heart has deceived you thus far, something is pulling at you that you must listen to. This might mean you are currently in a relationship you need to end as soon as possible. If this is you, let me first tell you it is okay—I promise things will be fine! I encourage you to take this to a trusted person to help you ascertain clear thinking. Maybe you do not need to end the relationship, but have some tough conversations. Do it!

Remember that you can even do this in a way that exalts Christ. Just because you break up, that does not mean you have failed. It actually means you have succeeded if breaking up brings the most glory to God. I am not saying it will be easy, but I am simply challenging you to act in faith. Take the risk. See what God does.

This might mean you are in a relationship that needs some drastic changes. Make those changes as soon as possible. Clearly define those changes and how they are going to take place. I will add that if you are a girl and are feeling this way, it is going to be a little more difficult. I suggest you talk to your boyfriend about these changes and see if he will lead in making them. If he refuses to do that, you have a very clear answer. If you are a guy, man up and lead. Just be sensitive and thoughtful as you go about navigating changes. Take the risk. See what God does.

This might mean you have been pursuing a person for a while and were so close to dating...until now. You might have realized some things about that person while reading this book that cause you to question if you really want to date or not. Give it more time. Make sure you are living in a window of being friends, and try to displace any emotions that might cloud your judgment. If time is not the answer, perhaps you need to let go of the idea of dating that person altogether. Take the risk. See what God does.

This might mean you have only confirmed the relationship you are in as one that honors Christ. Maybe there are some small tweaks to consider, but overall maybe things are right where they need to be. Strive to honor Christ, to continue in that godly relationship. View what you are in as something greater than just a dating relationship, but a light for the world to see as an example. Take the risk. See what God does.

The Relationship Lens

After all, is God not worth the risk? Is God's arm long enough to reach down and intervene in your life? Is God bigger than the relationship at hand? At the end of the day, your life is a beautiful and complicated painting. You are close up, looking on as the artist brushes strokes that are detailed, complex, and beautiful. Others who walk by see the picture of your life at a distance, and they notice how beautiful it is becoming. They see the parts not painted yet, and they wonder what the final piece will look like.

You, on the other hand, cannot see the painting as they can. Because you are so close to it, it is hard to even make out the picture. You sometimes only see the strange, black strokes of the brush and are saddened by how ugly they are. Sometimes you fail to see the blank spots of the painting that have yet to be filled in.

What I'm asking you to do is step back from the painting and take it all in. See how beautiful the picture of your life is becoming, and see what parts have not been painted yet. You are the masterpiece of all God's creation. The artist painting it is the Creator of the universe. He saw the completed picture in His mind before He even began the painting. You just need to trust that He is working you and your life into a magnificent piece, one stroke at a time. Just step back and enjoy the painting. With God orchestrating the brush strokes, you can trust and know the painting will turn out to be beautiful. Stop worrying about those seemingly ugly strokes you do not yet understand. Those strokes might not be as ugly as you think once the Creator is finished with them.

Act in faith. See what God does.

CPSIA information can be obtained at www.ICGtesting.com
Printed in the USA
LVOW08s0316150716

496224LV00005B/8/P